BUSH HATE

by
Thought Head

thoughthead@msn.com
http://thoughthead.blogspot.com

iUniverse, Inc.
New York   Bloomington

BUSH HATE

iUniverse books may be ordered through booksellers or by contacting:

iUniverse
1663 Liberty Drive
Bloomington, IN 47403
www.iuniverse.com
1-800-Authors (1-800-288-4677)

ISBN: 978-0-595-52807-3 (pbk)
ISBN: 978-0-595-62861-2 (ebk)

Printed in the United States of America

iUniverse rev. date 10/30/08

CONTENTS

Chapter 4   We are Ugly to the Rest of the World

Chapter 5   UK and USA

Chapter 6   How Liberals Think

Chapter 7   Addled Liberal Thinking

Chapter 8 Media

Chapter 9 Lies, Propaganda, Intelligence Failures

Chapter 10 Democracy Abroad and Security at Home

Chapter 11 Economy/Income/Tax

Chapter 12 Environment and Politics

Chapter 13 September 11 and its Aftermath

Chapter 14 War on Terrorism

Chapter 15 M-word

Chapter 16 Iraq

Chapter 17 Iran

Chapter 18 Looking Back

Chapter 19 Looking Forward

FOREWORD

The overriding question we face as a nation is what will we do when we no longer have Bush to kick around? We have little time left to address this question and to find a solution.

I was inspired to write on this topic by an Australian friend over dinner recently after I found that he had visited Cuba a few months ago but refused to visit the USA since he viewed us as the Evil Empire. I listened patiently while he extolled the virtues of the Cuban health care system while scoffing at the USA. But when I tried to correct the outrageous incorrect facts of him and two other friends, I was told that I was being much too dogmatic! A sample of the subjects I was forced to refute was that the Bush brothers conspired in Florida to steal the election from Al Gore. What is particularly galling is that all these incorrect old chestnut falsehoods had their origin from US Liberals. The upshot is that my self-righteous friends wanted me to stop supporting President Bush and the USA and admit that both are evil. If only I had done so, I would have had a much more pleasant dinner.

Hating the president is almost as old as the republic itself. Bush hatred, however, is openly endorsed as a virtue and enthusiastically proclaimed not only as a rational response to the President and his administration but also as a mark of morality. Liberals consider that Bush hatred is fully warranted by his theft of the 2000 election in Florida with the aid of the Supreme Court's decision in Bush v. Gore; his politicization of national security by making the overthrow of Saddam Hussein an issue in the 2002 midterm elections; and his shredding of the Constitution to authorize the torture of enemy combatants. Of course, these very examples illustrate nothing so much as the damage hatred inflicts on the rationality of the hater.

The facts are that in 2000 it was Al Gore who shifted the election controversy to the courts by filing a lawsuit challenging decisions made by local Florida county election supervisors. Moreover, between the Florida Supreme Court and the U.S. Supreme Court, 10 of 16 higher court judges -- five of whom were Democratic appointees -- found equal protection flaws with the recount scheme ordered by the intermediate Florida court. As for the 2002 midterm elections, aren't questions of war and peace proper ones to put to the people? From Liberal denunciations you would never know that the Bush administration has rejected torture as illegal. And in our system of government the executive branch, which has principal responsibility for defending the nation, is in wartime bound to overreach -- especially when it confronts on a daily basis intelligence reports that describe terrifying threats -- but that when checked by the Supreme Court the Bush administration has, in accordance with the system, promptly complied with the law.

Bush hatred is not a rational response to actual Bush perfidy. Rather, Bush hatred compels Liberals to reduce complicated events and multilayered issues to simple matters of good and evil. Bush hatred blinds Liberals to the other sides of the argument, and constrains the hater to see a monster instead of a political opponent.

Why do Liberals embrace all foreign oppressive governments as long as these oppose the West? One reason is that the death of communism has brought a dark liberation to Liberals in that they now feel free to champion any totalitarian group that is anti-western and anti-American. This mindset is particularly prevalent amongst self-styled intellectuals and the mass media.

CHAPTER 1
INTRODUCTION

Liberal Nihilism

Liberals have failed to confront attempted genocide in Bosnia, Kosovo, Israel and elsewhere in the Middle East, including Saddam's atrocities. Liberals are even confused about Saddam's arms suppliers. Between 1973 and 2002, 57 per cent of those weapons came from the Soviet Union/Russia, 13 per cent from France and 12 per cent from China. The USA and UK together did not contribute even one per cent.

The hate-filled and the irreconcilable do not disappear with geopolitical changes, so a revived radicalism was inevitable after the fall of the Berlin Wall. Even Khomeinian ayatollocracy is endorsed as it is against Western democracy. Alliances to-day and the behavior of the likes of George Galloway and Hezbollah are reminiscent of the infamous Hitler-Stalin pact in the 1930s. Some Liberals are so deluded that they have completely abandoned the values that once formed part of the democratic mainstream and have adopted a nihilistic culture steeped in hedonism and ignorance. That is why they embrace or excuse losers, demagogues and dictators like Mugabe and Chavez. It is not a large leap from marching in support of homicidal terrorists and sadistic Islamist and Baathist regimes to nurturing the loathsome anti-Semitism which motivates the moral inversion that they need in order to appear the champion of the victim. These Liberals desperately need to have faith of some sort, no matter how evil or psychotic, to persuade themselves that their paranoia about an American "theocracy" or a "Zionist conspiracy" is valid. They cling to their conspiracy theories so fervently that it is impossible for verifiable facts or reality to penetrate the bell jar of their lunacy. Their delusions shield them from the implications of the abject failure of their murderous ideology that has brought misery and death to millions.

The intensity of their projection derives from the need to believe that the latest manifestation of their bankrupt nihilistic collectivist ideology stands for peace and that the Conservatives/Christians/Zionists/Capitalists cause all the world's evil rather than their own grotesque behavior.

In their chosen role as the victims of America and Israel, these pampered elites congratulate themselves on their "courageous" and "principled" stand against "Western hegemony." They are thus not to blame for the terrifying emptiness within and the encroaching darkness of terrorism out there. Without Bush, the world would be a paradise. Externalizing the blame for their own unease is essential in order to deny the facts and banish the gnawing of reality.

The loathing of everything American erases any sense of moral perspective for power hungry and status seeking Liberals. They support the worst kind of anti-Westerners: racists, fascists, terrorists - anything goes as long as you're against America.

Liberal Hatred

Liberal hatred against Bush has become almost a celebration of Saddam's rule. In Michael Moore's Fahrenheit 9/11, pictures of pre-invasion Iraq are not real; the ethnic cleansing, the prison abuses, the rapes, the one-party-rule and Saddam's atrocities go entirely unmentioned. That Liberals could be against the war is understandable. That they could be so oblivious to Saddam Hussein is troubling.

The Liberal rationale is that the West is responsible for everything bad that happens anywhere in the world. The root of Terrorism is in the justified grievances of Palestinians, Saudis, Afghanis, etc, etc. Once these grievances would be assuaged, the problems in the Middle East: the Dictatorships, the Terrorist regimes, the extreme fundamentalists would go away.

Supporters of the Boycott of Israel will happily tell you all about the horrors of Israel's occupation of the West Bank, (while ignoring or excusing Palestinian terrorism), but they won't tell you what kind of criteria exists for boycotting Israel rather then the US, Russia, China or Sudan. This blatant racism is heralded by Liberals.

Liberals argue that Tony Blair and George Bush are the problem. Terrorists are "insurgents" against Anglo-American "imperialism." Liberals have become reflexively anti-American and anti-Israel. When Saddam was in power, they considered America his enabler, so they were against Saddam. After he was toppled, they supported the insurgents, and consider the Maliki government a version of the Vichy regime. They ignore the fact that the Maliki government is one of the most democratically elected in the Arab world.

British Liberals, under the pretense of multiculturalism, also make allowances for some of the most extremist Muslim views imaginable. Not understanding the practices of female genital mutilation, honor killings, wife-beating, suicide-bombing and so forth is succumbing to "Islamophobia." The left has forgotten that multiculturalism only works when its participants believe in a plurality of opinion, not when there are those who in principle deny others their opinions.

Liberals spend all their time excoriating Bush and Blair, and no time supporting the Iraqi people. Liberals constant maneuvering as the opposition party of Anglo-American policy and Israel has put it in untenable and dangerous contrarian positions. At least Blair is now safely out to pasture leaving Bush as the remaining bogeyman. He though is the main target. Blair, particularly in the eyes of British Liberals, was simply Bush's poodle.

What Has Happened to Leftist Passions?

In the past, leftist passion tended to show praiseworthy concern for the underdog. Liberals to-day often explicitly ignore the very victims that they used to support. They are absent when it comes to overthrowing tyrannical regimes and supporting civil liberties and freedoms. Amnesty International and Human Rights Watch have become perverted into opposing individual rights and freedoms.

Terrorism is not a side effect; it is the total system. When the pretensions of the workers' state or the thousand years Reich or the glorious union of Arabs are stripped away, when the differences between communism and fascism are forgotten, what remains is the sneer of the psychopathic killer who knows he's got the Liberals in his pocket.

Liberals have abandoned their former principles simply in order to side with those who oppose the United States (or the West in general). But it places much of the Liberal intelligentsia in firm opposition to truth, reconciliation and enlightened democracy. The fall of the Soviet Union and the end of Socialism as a viable option has much to do with the Liberals opposition to US capitalism and the USA as the only superpower. The USA is the new enemy.

Whatever it's causes are, the Liberal elite today know what they are against: America, the West and Israel, but is far less certain about what it is for - which allows it support the Ayatollah Regime in Iran, murderous Baathists in Iraq, Castro's dictatorship in Cuba and Kaddafi's in Libya: in short, everyone who is against the West.

The Enemy Within

Bush hate starts at home. US domestic politics dictates foreign policy and the main consideration is power in Washington. Few people in the USA are knowledgeable about the Middle East, including where it is geographically. Even fewer care about Iraq, but it was an excellent opportunity for Liberals to undermine the Republican government and to seize power since armed conflict is always messy with indeterminate consequences particularly short term. Liberals have no policies of their own but they are adept at creating conflict even if the result is to undermine US standing and prestige throughout the world.

United the USA does not stand. The United Nations would have us believe that we should all live as one happy family by talking through our differences. The historical reality is that one superpower has always been the world's policeman. In 1940, the baton was passed from Britain to a reluctant USA. Before then, Britain had ruled the world for several centuries and had stood alone against Hitler after French resistance collapsed in WW2. There were many Nazi sympathizers in the USA, notably the late Joe Kennedy, but Roosevelt eventually steered the USA into the war and from that time to the present the USA became leader and defender of the Free World.

Since then, the USA has performed this role with success and is the first superpower to have done so selflessly. Firstly Fascism was defeated and US money channeled to rebuild Germany and Japan. Socialism and Communism have been defeated. Terrorism will be defeated even though the conflict will be long against an invisible, amorphous enemy that attacks the innocent and most vulnerable and will stop at nothing.

Our real enemy is within our borders. However vile, everything that the rest of the world says about the USA and its leaders has been said by our own citizens first. US Liberals try to divide instead of standing united. They do not accept that they should support our President until the next election.

Hate in Politics

Major damage occurs when hate is directed against our President. The Liberals' hatred is so strong that they are seemingly indifferent to the consequences of portraying our elected Leader as a half wit. They are telling the world that we are all stupid in electing him and that he should be treated with contempt. Their hatred is based on lies about George Bush's IQ, integrity, character, oratory and beliefs. They insult not only George Bush, but more importantly the USA, since we chose him through our democratic processes. By so doing, they threaten the security and well being of all of us. The world community feels that they can treat us with contempt.

Blatant hate comments have been made by -

Cindy Sheehan, who denounced President Bush as an "evil maniac" and "Führer" and said his administration -- "the biggest terrorist outfit in the world" -- is committing "blatant genocide" in Iraq.

Syndicated cartoonist Pat Oliphant depicted Bush as imploring a cosmetic surgeon to make him "look like a leader" that the "herd" will "follow blindly and without question." The surgeon transforms him into a Hitler look-alike.

Senator Jim Jeffords of Vermont accused the Bush family of planning to "start another war . . . next year, probably in Iran" in order "to get their son" -- Florida Governor Jeb Bush -- "elected president" in the next election.

Harry Belafonte described black members of the Bush administration as "black tyrants" -- and added "Hitler had a lot of Jews high up in the hierarchy of the Third Reich."

Not all the hate is directed at George Bush -

"Black Democratic leaders in Maryland say that racially tinged attacks against Lt. Gov. Michael Steele, who is also black, . . . are fair because he is a conservative Republican," The Washington Times reported. "Such attacks . . . include pelting him with Oreo cookies during a campaign appearance, calling him an 'Uncle Tom,' and depicting him as a black faced minstrel."

University of Michigan historian Juan Cole, frequently on TV talk shows, asserted falsely that Middle East scholar Daniel Pipes "has fond visions of rounding up Muslim Americans and putting them in concentration camps."

Rabbi Eric Yoffie of the Union for Reformed Judaism compares Conservatives to Nazis. Just as the religious right today opposes same-sex marriage, Yoffie said last month, "we cannot forget that when Hitler came to power in 1933, one of the first things that he did was ban gay organizations."

Europe – Thy Name is Cowardice

Henry Broder wrote in Die Welt –

"Europe—your family name is appeasement." It's a phrase you can't get out of your head because it's so terribly true. Appeasement cost millions of Jews and non-Jews their lives as England and France, allies at the time, negotiated and hesitated too long before they noticed that Hitler had to be fought, not bound to toothless agreements. Appeasement legitimized and stabilized Communism in the Soviet Union, then East Germany, then all the rest of Eastern Europe where for decades, inhuman suppressive, murderous governments were glorified as the ideologically correct alternative to all other possibilities. Appeasement crippled Europe when genocide ran rampant in Kosovo, and even though we had absolute proof of ongoing mass-murder, we Europeans debated and debated and debated, and were still debating when finally the Americans had to come from halfway around the world, into Europe yet again, and do our work for us. Rather than protecting democracy in the Middle East, European appeasement, camouflaged behind the fuzzy word "equidistance", now countenances suicide bombings in Israel by fundamentalist Palestinians. Appeasement generates a mentality that allows Europe to ignore nearly 500,000 victims of Saddam's torture and murder machinery and, motivated by the self-righteousness of the peace-movement, has the gall to issue bad grades to George Bush … Even as it is uncovered that the loudest critics of the American action in Iraq made illicit billions, no, tens of billions, in the corrupt U.N. Oil-for-Food program. And now we are faced with a particularly grotesque form of appeasement. How is Germany reacting to the escalating violence by Islamic fundamentalists in Holland and elsewhere? By suggesting that we really should have a "Muslim Holiday" in Germany? I wish I were joking, but I am not. A substantial fraction of our (German) Government, and if the polls are to be believed, the German people, actually believe that creating an Official State "Muslim Holiday" will somehow spare us from the wrath of the fanatical Islamists. One cannot help but recall Britain's Neville Chamberlain waving the laughable treaty signed by Adolph Hitler, and declaring "European Peace in our time". What else has to happen before the European public and its political leadership get it? There is a sort of crusade underway, an especially perfidious crusade consisting of systematic attacks by fanatic Muslims, focused on civilians, directed against our free, open Western societies, and intent upon Western Civilization's utter destruction. It is a conflict that will most likely last longer than any of the great military conflicts of the last century—a conflict conducted by an enemy that cannot be tamed by "tolerance" and "accommodation" but is actually spurred on by such gestures, which have proven to be, and will always be taken by the Islamists for signs of weakness. Only two recent American

Presidents had the courage needed for anti-appeasement: Reagan and Bush.

His American critics may quibble over the details, but we Europeans know the truth. We saw it first hand: Ronald Reagan ended the Cold War, freeing half of the German people from nearly 50 years of terror and virtual slavery. And Bush, supported only by the Social Democrat Blair, acting on moral conviction, recognized the danger in the Islamic War against democracy. His place in history will have to be evaluated after a number of years have passed. In the meantime, Europe sits back with charismatic self-confidence in the multicultural corner, instead of defending liberal society's values and being an attractive center of power on the same playing field as the true great powers, America and China. On the contrary—we Europeans present ourselves, in contrast to those arrogant Americans", as the World Champions of "tolerance", which even (Germany's Interior Minister) Otto Schily justifiably criticizes. Why? Is it because we are so moral? I fear it's more because we're so materialistic and so devoid of a moral compass. For his policies, Bush risks the fall of the dollar, huge amounts of additional national debt, and a massive and persistent burden on the American economy—because unlike almost all of Europe, Bush realizes what is at stake—literally everything.

While we criticize the "capitalistic robber barons" of America because they seem too sure of their priorities, we timidly defend our Social Welfare systems. Stay out of it! It could get expensive! We'd rather discuss reducing our 35-hour workweek or our dental coverage, or our 4 weeks of paid vacation … Or listen to TV pastors preach about the need to "reach out to terrorists. To understand and forgive". These days, Europe reminds me of an old woman who, with shaking hands, frantically hides her last pieces of jewelry when she notices a robber breaking into a neighbor's house.

America Alone

In the ongoing conflict between the West and Islam, both the demographics and the will to power favor the Islamists -

That a country like Spain, with a birth rate of 1.15 children per adult women, will extinguish itself in a few generations, while immigrants from countries such as Pakistan (birth rate 4.53) will move in to fill the vacuum.

That as an aggressive, unassimilated minority edges closer to a majority (as in France, with an estimated 30% Muslim population in the under 20 age group), the character of the democratic institutions will become more closely aligned with Islamic law and culture.

That the decline in Christianity and the welfare state is largely to blame for the pessimism and failures of will demonstrated by Europe.

That America represents the primary exception to this trend, if only by degree and that only a concerted effort to save our society stands a chance of reversing these trends.

Anti-Bush in Bridge

In the genteel world of bridge, disputes are usually handled quietly and rarely involve issues of national policy. In a protest reminiscent of an anti-Bush statement by the pop group Dixie Chicks in 2003, a team of women who represented the United States at the world bridge championships in Shanghai scribbled on the back of a menu, that was held up at an awards dinner, "We did not vote for Bush." By e-mail, angry bridge players have accused the women of "treason" and "sedition." They are facing sanctions, including a yearlong ban from competition. The action by the team, which had won the Venice Cup, the women's title, at the Shanghai event, could cost the federation corporate sponsors.

The players decided to put up the sign in response to negative comments from players from other countries about American interrogation techniques, the war in Iraq and other foreign policy issues, saying "There was a lot of anti-Bush feeling, questioning of our Iraq policy and about torture."

Robert S. Wolff, one of the country's pre-eminent bridge players, who has served as an executive and board member of several bridge organizations, said that he understood that the women might have had a legal right to do what they did but that they had offended many people. "While I believe in the right to free speech, to me that doesn't give anyone the right to criticize one's leader at a foreign venue in a totally nonpolitical event."

CHAPTER 2
A HISTORICAL
PERSPECTIVE

Ungrateful Europe

What has the USA done for the world? The USA has repeatedly saved Europe from itself. The USA was a critical factor in ending World War 1 and the key factor in winning World War 2. The USA then defeated communism.

The USA joined WW1 on April 2nd, 1917. The war lasted from August 4, 1914 to November 11, 1918. It involved many of the countries of Europe as well the United States and other nations throughout the world. More than 10 million people were killed and more than 20 million wounded. The breakdown of old alliances among European powers and an arms race led by Germany helped set the stage for the conflict, which was sparked by the assassination of Archduke Ferdinand of Austria in 1914. Hostilities began on August 4, 1914 when Germany invaded Belgium. The Allied Powers (led by Britain, France, and the United States) defeated the Central Powers (led by Germany, Austria-Hungary, and the Ottoman Empire). Allied Power Russia left the war after the Russian Revolution of 1917, the same year that the USA entered the war. The war ended the German Empire, the Austro-Hungarian Empire, Ottoman Empire, and the Russian Empire. The Treaty of Versailles (1919) severely punished Germany as the alleged instigator of the war.

Even though World War I started in 1914, token American forces of 27,000 were first deployed only at the end of 1917. In early 1918, entire divisions were beginning to serve on the front lines alongside French troops. American forces first saw serious action during the summer of 1918, contributing eight large divisions, alongside 24 French ones, at the Second Battle of the Marne. Along with the Fourth Army's victory at Amiens, the Franco-American victory at the Second Battle of the Marne marked a turning point of the war on the Western Front.

The outbreak of civil unrest and naval mutiny in Germany, the collapse of Bulgaria, Turkey and particularly Austria-Hungary following Allied victories in Salonika, Syria and Italy, and the Allied victories on the Western Front were among a series of events in the autumn of 1918 which made it clear that Allied victory was inevitable, and diplomatic inquiries about an armistice had been going on throughout October. The U.S. breakout from the Argonne at the start of November was a decisive event leading to the German acceptance of an armistice, because it made untenable the Antwerp-Meuse line.

By the end of the war, U.S. troop strength in Europe (1.9 million) was slightly greater than that of the British Expeditionary Forces (1.7m). French strength (three Army Groups, totaling 2.5m) was still greater, but much of it was deployed in quiet sectors such as Alsace, and after horrendous casualties and mutiny earlier in the war, France was only able or willing to undertake major offensives in conjunction with U.S. troops. The threat of ever-greater U.S. commitment was another factor driving the German leadership to ask for an armistice.

Lend-Lease in World War 2

On March 11 1941, President Roosevelt signed into law the Lend-Lease Bill, providing war supplies to countries fighting the Axis.

Lend-Lease was the name of the program under which the United States of America supplied Great Britain, the Soviet Union, China, France and other Allied nations with vast amounts of war material (matériel) between 1941 and 1945. It began in March 1941, nine months before Pearl Harbor. It ended soon after V-J Day, on 2 September 1945.

A total of $50.1 billion worth of supplies were shipped: $31.4 billion to Britain, $11.3 billion to the Soviet Union, $3.2 billion to France and $1.6 billion to China. Reverse Lend Lease comprised services (like rent on air bases) that went to the U.S. It totaled $7.8 billion, of which $6.8 billion came from the Britain and the Commonwealth. Apart from that, there were no repayments of supplies that arrived before the termination date. (Supplies after that date were sold to Britain at a 75% discount, or $650 million, using long-term loans from the U.S.) No lend lease money went to Canada, which operated a similar program that sent $4.7 billion in supplies to Britain and Soviet Union.

In contrast to the American loans to the Allies in World War I, there were no provisions for postwar repayments.

The Marshall Plan

The Marshall Plan, officially the European Recovery Program (ERP), was the primary plan of the United States for rebuilding the allied countries of Europe and repelling communism after World War II. The initiative was named for United States Secretary of State George Marshall and was largely the creation of State Department officials, especially William L. Clayton and George F. Kennan.

The reconstruction plan was developed at a meeting of the participating European states on July 12 1947. The Marshall Plan offered the same aid to the Soviet Union and its allies, if they would make political reforms and accept certain outside controls. The plan was in operation for four years beginning in July 1947. During that period some $13 billion of economic and technical assistance was given to help the recovery of the European countries that had joined in the Organization for Economic Co-operation and Development.

By the time the plan had come to completion, the economy of every participant state had grown well past pre-war levels. Over the next two decades, many regions of Western Europe would enjoy unprecedented growth and prosperity. The Marshall Plan has also long been seen as one of the first elements of European integration, as it erased tariff trade barriers and set up institutions to coordinate the economy on a continental level.

Truman Doctrine

On March 12 1947, President Truman established what became known as the Truman Doctrine to help Greece and Turkey resist Communism.

The Truman Doctrine was a United States foreign policy designed to contain Communism by stopping its spread to Greece and Turkey. President Harry S. Truman proclaimed the Doctrine on March 12, 1947. It stated that the U.S. would support Greece and Turkey with economic and military aid to prevent their falling into the Soviet orbit. The Doctrine shifted American foreign policy towards the Soviet Union from Détente to a policy of containment of Soviet expansion and so was the starting date of the Cold War.

Harry Truman decision, supported by the Republican-controlled Congress, came after the United Kingdom urgently informed Washington that it was no longer able to support the Greek government's efforts to fight its civil war against Communist insurgents (1946-1949). Aid was given to Turkey because of the historic tensions with Greece. It was an early response to political aggression by the Soviet Union in Europe and the Middle East, illustrated through the Communist movements in Turkey and Greece. The Truman Doctrine was the first in a succession of containment moves by the United States, followed by economic restoration of Western Europe through the The Marshall Plan and military containment by the creation of NATO in 1949. In Truman's words, it became "the policy of the United States to support free peoples who are resisting attempted subjugation by armed minorities or by outside pressures." Truman reasoned, because these "totalitarian regimes" coerced "free peoples," they represented a threat to international peace and the national security of the United States.

President Truman made the proclamation in an address to the U.S. Congress on March 12, 1947, amid the crisis of the Greek Civil War (1946-1949). Truman insisted that if Greece and Turkey did not receive the aid that they needed, they would inevitably fall to communism with consequences throughout the region.

Truman signed the act into law on May 22, 1947, which granted $400 million ($350 million to Greece and $50 million to Turkey) in military and economic aid. The economic aid was to be used in repairing the infrastructure of these countries and military aid came in the form of military personnel supervising and helping with the reconstruction of these countries while training soldiers. This aid was to help Greece and Turkey get back on their feet so they could both support and defend themselves from coercive forces.

This American aid was in many ways a replacement for British aid which the British were no longer financially in a position to give. The policy of containment and opposition to communists in Greece for example was carried out by the British before 1947 in many of the same ways it was carried out afterward by the Americans.

Fighting Communism

On December 16, 1950, President Truman proclaimed a national state of emergency in order to fight "Communist imperialism." The April 1950 "NSC-68" policy paper overturned the previous balanced and prudent approach to the Cold War and prepared the way for a dramatic militarization of U.S. foreign policy, aimed against the Soviet Union and the People's Republic of China. The paper called for massive increases in defense spending and building capabilities for fighting "limited wars" in peripheral areas around the globe.

Soviet policy was presented as nothing more than an absolute determination to spread the Communist system throughout the world. In fact, the Soviet Union was largely motivated by its interests as a national state.

The previous concept of patient long-term "containment," emphasizing political, economic, diplomatic, and psychological means, was replaced by an aggressive policy emphasizing military confrontation. The Marshall Plan itself then became militarized, contrary to its original spirit.

The Korean War, launched in June 1950 by North Korea, triggered the critical escalation of the Cold War and the conversion of the United States into a "national security state," or "garrison state," as President Eisenhower called it. Stalin and Mao gave a "green light," to be sure, but it was a North Korean initiative and a Korean civil war. It was not part of a Stalinist blueprint for world conquest and World War III. There was little chance of the Soviet Union's repeating the invasion in any other place, such as Germany. The Soviet action in Korea was limited strictly to Korea.

Nevertheless, the Korean War was interpreted by Acheson and most others in the State Department, as well as the Joint Chiefs of Staff, as ushering in a new phase of Soviet foreign policy. Their view, which Truman accepted, was that having launched an attack on Korea—the first case of Communist open use of naked military force to expand the system—the Soviet Union was likely to call on satellite armies elsewhere, particularly in East Germany, to spread Communist control.

The Liberal faction in Washington was quick to take advantage of the North Korean attack to impose its will on U.S. foreign policy through the manipulation of fear and the creation of an atmosphere of crisis and emergency. Indeed, U.S. military forces under MacArthur's arrogant leadership recklessly crossed the 38th parallel and approached China's borders. After a due official diplomatic warning from China via India and multiple other diplomatic avenues, the Chinese eventually sent some 400,000 troops against U.S. forces. Overall some 2.5 million Chinese military and some 500,000 Chinese civilians would serve in the Korean War to counter MacArthur's threatening behavior.

The Korean War was immediately painted by the Liberal faction as a demonstration of Soviet global designs and a step in its master plan for world domination and even "World War III." At the same time, a potentially viable U.S. policy option for easing mainland China away from the Soviet bloc by normalizing our relations with Beijing, and developing commercial relations, was dropped.

Although the United Kingdom, and a number of other countries, quickly developed relations with Beijing, the United States pressured Japan, and other countries, to refrain from so doing. The People's Republic of China was treated by Washington as a "pariah state" or "rogue state."

Washington appointed itself the savior of human freedom and endowed itself with worldwide responsibility and a worldwide charter ... the guardianship of world freedom required, first of all, an enormous military establishment.... The new American approach to world affairs, the obsession with crisis, the illusion of "world leadership," the obligations of duty so intertwined with the opportunities of power carried forward the process, begun during the Second World War, of elevating "national security" into a national obsession of saving the world from Communism.

The fear mongering and military build up which was part of the Truman Administration took the United States in the wrong direction culminating in the disaster of Vietnam.

Tear Down This Wall

On June 12, 1987, President Reagan, during a visit to the divided German city of Berlin, publicly challenged Soviet leader Mikhail S. Gorbachev to "tear down this wall."

Speaking 100 yards from the wall that was thrown up in 1961 to thwart an exodus to the West, Mr. Reagan made the wall a metaphor for ideological and economic differences separating East and West.

"There is one sign the Soviets can make that would be unmistakable, that would advance dramatically the cause of freedom and peace," the President said.

"Secretary General Gorbachev, if you seek peace - if you seek prosperity for the Soviet Union and Eastern Europe - if you seek liberalization: come here, to this gate. "Mr. Gorbachev, open this gate. "Mr. Gorbachev, tear down this wall."

Mr. Reagan made the remarks with the Brandenburg Gate in East Berlin in the background. An East Berlin security post was in view.

On October 18, 1989, East German leader Erich Honecker resigned, and on November 9, East Germany's new leadership eased restrictions on East Germans leaving the country, effectively marking the fall of the Berlin Wall.

Reagan's resolute opposition to Soviet hegemony was a major factor in the overthrow of Communist regimes that occurred in the two years immediately following his presidency.

Communism was soundly defeated by Capitalism.

A comparison with President Lincoln

We have the capability to win in the Middle East. The only question is whether we have the resolve.

At the start of the Civil War, many Northerners anticipated a quick victory. The New York Times predicted victory in 30 days. By 1863, the war was being denounced in Congress as an utter, disastrous, and most bloody failure, while President Lincoln and his administration were despised for their incompetence. "There never was such a shambling, half-and-half set of incapables collected in one government, before or since the world began," a Liberal senator said in disgust.

Why then does the USA hold President Lincoln in such high esteem to-day?

Just as then, we have to choose between resolve and retreat, with no guarantees about how it will end. All we can be sure of is that the stakes once again are liberty and decency versus tyranny and terror. We are fighting an enemy that feeds on weakness and expects us to lose heart. The world for generations to come will remember if we flinch.

Iraq Recent History

In 1983, President Reagan initiated a strategic alliance with Iraq, then in the third year of a war of attrition with neighboring Iran. Although Iraq had started the war with a blitzkrieg attack in 1980, the tide had turned by 1982 in favor of much larger Iran, and the Reagan administration was afraid Iraq might actually lose.

The Reagan administration believed that Hussein could be a strategic partner to the United States, a counterweight to Iran, a force for moderation in the region, and possibly help in the Arab-Israel peace process.

US policy towards Saddam Hussein changed dramatically when he attacked and occupied Kuwait, threatening Saudi Arabia and other strategic allies in the Middle East.

Naive Liberals have great difficulty in understanding the reasons for these policy changes. They do not understand the shifting sands of world politics and think that do good diplomacy under the guise of our more enlightened, superior democratic culture is the antidote to all problems everywhere. Jimmy Carter polishes his credentials at home with a hammer in hand as he poses for a photo shoot at a Habitat for Humanity House under construction. He then leads US Liberals in his mistaken crusade worldwide with his superior vision, blinding him to the reality on the ground around him. His latest gaffe is his recent meeting with the leader of Hamas.

CHAPTER 3
FAMILY VALUES

Bush Family

When I visited the Library of George Bush Senior, what struck me most forcibly was what a thoroughly decent person he is and how the Bush family back to his grandparents and Barbara's grandparents are all highly principled people with exemplary family values. As the Senior George Bush described his own father - he gave us love and discipline in equal amounts and a great deal of both.

The Kennedy family, in contrast to the Bush family, is and always has been most dysfunctional.

Kennedy Family

In 1912 Joseph Kennedy married Rose Fitzgerald, the daughter of John F. Fitzgerald, the Democrat mayor of Boston and most recognized politician in the city.

He had an affair with Gloria Swanson during 1929 and 1930, during which time he poured large sums of money into Gloria Productions Limited, a film company which Swanson had just started.

In 1923 he set up his own investment company and became a multi-millionaire during the bull market of the 1920s. Kennedy formed alliances with several other Irish-Catholic money men, including Charles E. Mitchell, Michael J. Meehan and Bernard Smith. He helped establish the Libby-Owens-Ford stock pool, an arrangement in which Kennedy and colleagues created an artificial scarcity of Libby-Owens-Ford stock to drive up the value of their own holdings in the stock. Using inside information, and the public's lack of knowledge, a pool operator would bribe journalists to present that information in the most advantageous manner. The stocks would then change in price up or down depending on the position favoured by the pool. These market manipulations were in part responsible for the Stock Market Crash of 1929 which triggered the Great Depression.

Kennedy got out of the market in 1928, before the Crash locking in multi-million dollar profits. When the 1929 crash came, he added to his wealth by using short positions.

During Prohibition, Kennedy's company Somerset Importers became the exclusive American agent for Gordon's Dry Gin and Dewar's Scotch which was only allowed to be imported legally during Prohibition for medicinal purposes. Anticipating the end of Prohibition (not difficult to do as it slowly passed through the required number of states) he assembled a very large inventory of stock that he sold for a profit of millions of dollars when Prohibition was repealed in 1933. He invested this money in residential and commercial real estate, the Merchandise Mart in Chicago and Hialeah Race Track in Florida.

Kennedy made money from reorganizing and refinancing several Hollywood studios. He enjoyed the industry because of the attractive women involved in it.

In 1938, he was appointed as the United States Ambassador to Britain and was a Nazi sympathizer. He rejected the warnings by Winston Churchill that Nazi Germany posed a looming threat. He had to resign in September, 1940, because he disagreed with Roosevelt's policy of hostility toward Germany.

Joseph McCarthy after 1950 was the nation's most prominent Irish-American along with Kennedy. McCarthy became close friends with Kennedy, who contributed to McCarthy, and became one of his major supporters.

Kennedy was the power behind the throne in grooming, financing and managing his second son, John F. Kennedy to become President of the US in 1960.

Liberals Condemn President Bush but Revere President Kennedy

On November 8, 1960, Massachusetts Senator John F. Kennedy defeated Vice President Richard M. Nixon for the presidency.

Senator John F. Kennedy of Massachusetts finally won the 1960 Presidential election from Vice President Nixon by the astonishing margin of less than two votes per voting precinct.

Senator Kennedy's electoral vote total stood yesterday at 300, just thirty-one more than the 269 needed for election. The Vice President's total was 185. Fifty-two additional electoral votes, including California's thirty-two, were still in doubt last night.

But the popular vote was a different story. The two candidates ran virtually even. Senator Kennedy's lead last night was little more than 300,000 in a total tabulated vote of about 66,000,000 cast in 165,826 precincts.

That was a plurality for the Senator of less than one-half of 1 per cent of the total vote--the smallest percentage difference between the popular votes of two Presidential candidates since 1880, when James A. Garfield outran Gen. Winfield Scott Hancock by 7,000 votes in a total of almost 9,000,000.

Nevertheless, yesterday's voting radically altered the political balance of power in America in favor of the Democrats and put them in a commanding position in the Federal and state capitals unknown since the heyday of Franklin D. Roosevelt.

They regained control of the White House for the first time since 1952 and thus ended divided government in Washington. They retained control of the Senate and the House of Representatives, although with slightly reduced margins. And they increased their hold on the state governorships by one, bringing the Democratic margin to 34-16.

In addition to being one of the closest in American history, the election also saw some of the most virulent campaign tactics ever used. To the day he died, Nixon privately maintained that the election had been stolen by the strong-arm tactics of the Kennedy campaign. Indeed the result of this election placed Nixon on a collision course with the scandal of Watergate. After being steamrolled by a Kennedy campaign that had been willing to do anything to get elected, Nixon vowed never again to be caught off guard by such aggressive tactics, even if it meant breaking the law, just as Nixon felt the Kennedy people had done to win the election.

Kennedy's appetite for illicit sex was legendary. At the time of the election, Chicago mafia boss Sam Giancana, who shared a mistress with Kennedy, bragged that Kennedy wouldn't even be in the White House without the use of intimidation at the polls in Illinois.

Chicago mayor Richard Daley famously told Kennedy late on Election Day: "With a little bit of luck, and the help of a few close friends, you're going to carry Illinois."

The turnout in Chicago was a staggering 89% - compared to the national figure of 62.8%. And despite losing 93 of Illinois's 102 counties, Kennedy was eventually declared the winner by 8,858 votes.

As well as in Illinois, dirty tricks were alleged in several states including Missouri, Texas, New Jersey and West Virginia.

Chicago mayor Richard Daley famously told Kennedy late on Election Day: "With a little bit of luck, and the help of a few close friends, you're going to carry Illinois."

The turnout in Chicago was a staggering 89% - compared to the national figure of 62.8%. And despite losing 93 of Illinois's 102 counties, Kennedy was eventually declared the winner by 8,858 votes.

As well as in Illinois, dirty tricks were alleged in several states including Missouri, Texas, New Jersey and West Virginia.

The Kennedy Administration

The 1961 Bay of Pigs Invasion was an unsuccessful United States-planned and funded attempted invasion by armed Cuban exiles in southwest Cuba. An attempt to overthrow the government of Fidel Castro, this action accelerated a rapid deterioration in Cuban-American relations, which was further worsened by the Cuban Missile Crisis the following year.

Tensions between The United States and Cuba had increased steadily since the Cuban Revolution of 1959. A communist state was unwelcome mere miles away from the American mainland. The Eisenhower and Kennedy administrations had judged that Castro's policies, including the expropriation of US assets on the island and Cuba's increasing ties with the Soviet Union, could not be tolerated.

On March 17, 1960, the Eisenhower administration agreed to a recommendation from the CIA to equip and drill Cuban exiles for action against the new Castro government. Eisenhower stated that it was the policy of the U.S. government to aid anti-Castro guerilla forces. The CIA began to recruit and train anti-Castro forces in the Sierra Madre mountains on the Pacific coast of Guatemala.

On February 17, 1961, Kennedy, the new U.S. president, asked his advisors whether the toppling of Castro might be related to weapon shipments and if it was possible to claim the real targets were modern fighter aircraft and rockets which endangered America's security. At the time, Cuba's army possessed Soviet tanks, artillery and small arms, and its air force consisted of B-26 medium bombers, Hawker Sea Furies (a fast and effective, though obsolete, propeller driven fighter-bomber) and T-33 jets left over from the Batista Air Force.

In April 1961 the new Kennedy administration arranged for a force of CIA-trained Cuban exiles opposed to Castro to be landed at the Bay of Pigs. The invasion was quickly defeated by Cuba's military forces. Castro was then convinced the U.S. would invade Cuba. Shortly after routing the Bay of Pigs Invasion, he declared Cuba a socialist republic and established formal ties with the Soviet Union. The failed Bay of Pigs invasion severely embarrassed the Kennedy administration, and made Castro wary of future US intervention in Cuba. As a result of the failure, CIA director Allen Dulles, deputy CIA director Charles Cabell, and Deputy Director of Operations Richard Bissell were all forced to resign. All three were held responsible for the planning of the operation at the CIA. Responsibility of the Kennedy Administration and the US State Department for modifications of the plans was not apparent until later.

The CIA wrote a detailed internal report that laid blame for the failure squarely on internal incompetence. A number of grave errors by the CIA and other American analysts contributed to the debacle:

- The administration believed that the troops could retreat to the mountains to lead a guerrilla war if they lost in open battle. The mountains were too far to reach on foot, and the troops were deployed in swamp land, where they were easily surrounded.
- They believed that the involvement of the US in the incident could be denied.
- They believed that Cubans would be grateful to be liberated from Fidel Castro and would quickly join the battle. This support failed to materialize; many hundreds of thousands of others were arrested, and some executed, prior to the landings.

The Kennedy administration continued covert operations against Castro, later launching the Cuban Project to "help Cuba overthrow the Communist regime". Tensions would again peak in the Cuban Missile Crisis of 1962 which was the closest that the Cold War came to becoming a nuclear war.

The actual confrontation began on October 14, 1962, when U.S. reconnaissance photographs taken by an American U-2 spy plane revealed missile bases being built in Cuba, in response to similar U.S. bases built at the Turkish-Soviet border. On October 22 1962, President Kennedy announced an air and naval blockade of Cuba.

The crisis was defused when, after a bellicose confrontation on October 28, 1962, both U.S. President John F. Kennedy and Soviet General Secretary Nikita Khrushchev, with the intercession of U.N. Secretary-General, U Thant, agreed to remove their respective nuclear missiles.

The CIA admitted in documents released in 2007 on its Web site that they attempted to kill Fidel Castro during the Kennedy Administration. A 1965 Pentagon memorandum suggests that Jack and Bobby discussed and apparently sanctioned the development of a possible assassination attempt against Fidel Castro during a 1962 meeting in the Oval Office. The scheme they considered involved Ernest Hemingway's farm outside Havana.

President Kennedy and his brother the Attorney General wanted Fidel Castro out of the way. After Castro thwarted the Kennedy-approved and CIA-orchestrated invasion at the Bay of Pigs in April 1961, the Kennedys continued to seek means of toppling the Cuban leader. In early 1962, according to a CIA memo, Bobby Kennedy told a group of CIA and Pentagon officials that a solution to the Cuban problem carried "the top priority in the United States government--all else is secondary." Soon after, the CIA began devising a variety of assassination plans--efforts that would involve an exploding seashell, poison pills, a toxin-contaminated diving suit and Mafia associates. Ever since this clandestine activity started becoming public in the 1970s, former CIA officers have maintained that John and Robert Kennedy were fully aware of and supportive of the agency's lethal intentions, that the CIA conspirators were not rogues but loyal civil servants following orders.

Dial Joe-4-Chávez

The new generation of Kennedys is just as unprincipled.

The Boston Herald has stated that "entities related to his Citizens Energy Corp. paid Joe Kennedy more than $400,000 in 2003, the last year for which records are available." That is not bad for a non-profit executive willing to lend his name to a $9 million foreign disinformation campaign.

Joe is a partner of Chavez, the ally of the Iranian mullahs, a supporter of North Korea, a close friend of Fidel Castro and a good customer for Vladimir Putin's weapon factories.

The former Democratic Congressman describes the deal he's cooked up with Mr. Chávez as charity for low-income consumers of heating oil. But it's worth asking what the price of this largesse is to Venezuelans and to U.S. security interests.

Mr. Chavez's CITGO -- a Houston-based oil company owned by the Venezuelan government -- is supplying home heating oil to Mr.

Kennedy's Citizens Energy Corporation at a 40% discount. Citizens, a nonprofit outfit, say it passes the savings onto the poor, aiming to help 400,000 homes in 16 states that would otherwise have trouble heating their homes. In the process, Mr. Kennedy happens to get a high-profile publicity plug. If you think you qualify, says the television ad that drew our attention to this partnership, just dial 1-877-Joe-4-Oil.

Generous Joe is not the only one polishing his public image here. In the mold of the Castro strategy of sending armies of "doctors" and "teachers" among the Latin American poor, Mr. Chávez is trying to shape U.S. public opinion in the hope that more gringos will come to see the Chávez government as benevolent.

Massachusetts Democrats seem especially eager to help. In a September 29, 2005, "confidential memorandum" addressed to "President Hugo Chávez" and uncovered by a Congressional committee, William Delahunt (D., Mass.) gushed that it was a "pleasure" to have met with the strongman "to discuss your generous offer." The Democrat advised Mr. Chávez to steer his oil through Mr. Kennedy's nonprofit and declared that "from a public relations perspective" the discount oil scheme "is an extraordinary opportunity to address urgent needs of people living in poverty, while showcasing the compassion of your nation."

If fighting poverty is the goal, Mr. Delahunt would do better to remind Mr. Chávez that charity begins at home. The U.S. is far richer than Venezuela and since Hurricane Hugo took power in 1999 Venezuelan living standards have suffered despite soaring oil prices. Annual inflation averaged more than 20% between 2001 and 2005, imposing a tax on the poorest. Meanwhile, an insecure investment climate has taken a harsh toll on private-sector employment and shrunk the middle class.

In his eight years in power, Mr. Kennedy's business partner has also polarized Venezuela with his class warfare, rewritten the constitution, politicized the judiciary, the electoral council and military, and wants to make himself a dictator for life. Freedom House now ranks Venezuela 34th out of 35 countries in the Western Hemisphere in press freedom. Only the Cuban press is more repressed.

Transparency International puts Venezuela second to last in the Hemisphere in its 2006 "corruption perception index." And then there was that revealing rant against President Bush ("the devil") at the United Nations in September.

But Mr. Kennedy keeps on trucking. He defended his Chávez subsidy deal as "morally righteous," arguing that the CITGO contribution to his nonprofit is only "one-half of one percent" of CITGO oil and product sales in the U.S.

Mr. Kennedy said that Mr. Chávez has done "so much more" for the poor than any previous government. As for democracy, he said there was "ample room for improvement in the ways that people get elected in Venezuela as well as in Florida." Mr. Chávez chose his partner well.

U.S. Representative Patrick Kennedy

Patrick Kennedy, son of Ted, is one of the leading recipients of campaign contributions from Indian tribes represented by Jack Abramoff, the lobbyist who has pleaded guilty to corruption charges.

From 1999 through last year, the Rhode Island Democrat and his political action committee received $42,500 in contributions from a half-dozen tribes represented by Abramoff.

Kennedy has no plans to return the tribal campaign contributions. Indeed, Kennedy has received money from Indian tribes interested in gambling for much of his career. He was a founder of the Native American Caucus in the House of Representatives, and has received contributions from 110 tribes, many more than Abramoff tapped into

During his first term, Kennedy backed an effort by the Narragansett tribe to create a high-stakes gambling hall in Rhode Island. And as chairman of the Democratic Congressional Campaign Committee in 1999 and 2000, Kennedy helped Democratic House candidates raise money from various tribes.

Why is none of this information a surprise? What we have here is yet another Kennedy who knows how to tap into a rich source of other people's money. Indian tribes have a monopoly on gambling establishments because Liberals feel guilty about the way they were treated by the early settlers. To assuage this guilt, these profits from other people's gambling addictions are tax free. Republicans want to change that and so White Knight Patrick rides up to fight on their behalf, enriching himself at the same time. It is a variant of the same business model that Citizen Joe Kennedy uses in his non-profit Citizen's Energy (Joe gives away our tax dollars, Citizen's Energy pays no taxes and Joe pays himself handsomely).

Patrick Kennedy is not helping poverty stricken, welfare and liquor dependant Indians on their reservations. Instead he is enabling their behavior, while the beneficiaries of Indian gambling are insiders and power brokers like himself who siphon off the profits.

What brought Abramoff down was because he could not resist gloating in private emails, obtained by federal investigators. He described tribal leaders in one e-mail as "moronic," adding: "I'd love us to get our mitts on that moola!! Oh well, stupid folks get wiped out."

Yes – by Abramoff, Kennedy and many others who tap into that moola as they take advantage of vulnerable, uneducated and dependant people. These people have been made dependant by Liberal do-gooders with free hand outs of our tax dollars, instead of being taught tough love, self-help initiatives.

Indians' per capita income is less than $8,000 per year. Tribal gaming is a $19 billion industry, involving 228 tribes operating 405 gambling operations in 30 states. Patrick Kennedy takes money from almost half of these tribes and has done nothing to help poverty stricken Indians. As Alexis Johnson, a lawyer opposed to legalization of tribal gaming puts it "Lobbyists, legislators and inside-the-Beltway lawyers are the real stakeholders in Indian gambling". Patrick Kennedy is following in his grandfather's footsteps.

At a roast in 2002, Patrick Kennedy, the admitted former cokehead joked about Senator Lincoln Chafee (R-R.I.), another admitted former cokehead: "Now when I hear someone talking about a Rhode Island politician whose father was a senator and who got to Washington on his family name, used cocaine, and wasn't very smart, I know there is only a 50-50 chance it's me.

Chapter 4
We are Ugly to the Rest of the World

Ugly US Liberals

Whenever the leader of another country is visiting the White House, his treatment by the US Liberal Media is always the same. He stands there ignored while the President is asked questions that are intended to embarrass him and have nothing to do with our visitor.

The same happens when an American political leader is abroad – but in reverse. Condoleezza Rice was embarrassed by the US Liberal Media in every European country she visited, with her counterpart from that country standing silently by her side.

Do American Liberals really think that we are so much more important than any other country that they do not even need to show any interest in that country? How ignorant! How ugly!

The nasty treatment of Senator John McCain by faculty and students during his commencement address at the New School in New York shows that the ugly behavior of the Liberal media works with people who do not know how to behave and do not have minds of their own. These mindless sheep think that their rudeness is clever,

The ugliness toward Senator McCain reveals the pathetic rage that is now the hallmark of many Liberals. Dozens of faculty and students turned their back on the Senator, others booed and heckled, and a senior invited to speak threw out her prepared remarks and mocked their invited guest as he sat nearby. The Senator who spent years in the Hanoi Hilton reacted with admirable restraint to these insults. Liberals cannot forget the humiliation they created in Vietnam, which is when the seeds of the current antiwar rage were planted. Because of them the USA will never be a respected world power.

As predicted Condoleezza Rice was also insulted in the same way as Senator McCain at Boston College. It is clear that these graduating seniors did not learn how to behave from their parents or from their schools. Most probably did not learn much else that was positive either to prepare them to be world citizens. Instead they graduated as Ugly Americans. In her speech, Condoleezza Rice exhorted students to find a passion and pursue it. She advised them to use reason and compassion in navigating life and to work to advance human progress. The audience responded enthusiastically when Rice described her upbringing as an emblem of triumph over pessimism. "I grew up in Birmingham, Ala., the Birmingham of Bull Connor and the Ku Klux Klan, a place that was once quite properly described as the most segregated city in America. I know how it feels to hold aspirations when half your neighbors think that you're incapable or uninterested in anything higher," said Rice, the first black woman to hold her office.

Condoleezza Rice is an exceptionally talented woman with impressive accomplishments. It was quite a coup for a second rate college to persuade her to be their commencement speaker particularly as so few blacks and relatively few women have aspired to or succeeded in achieving so much. Ugly Liberal Americans though do not understand, but they do make a lot of noise.

The TV media has had a field day of Ugliness over the Aruba affair. The mother of the victim has become an Ugly American celebrity. The Arubans are portrayed as idiots and beach bums who prey on lovely, innocent American teenage cheerleaders, or as people devoid of all the skills (joke) of US Law Enforcement. For all the media coverage, no one has ever asked the questions about what the chaperones were doing, what the victim's friends were doing, what substances had the victim willingly consumed and why did she go on to the beach without her friends and with three males that she did not know. The tragedy itself and its aftermath typify Ugly American behavior.

The Duke Lacrosse Case

Liberals enjoy trying and besmirching WASPS (White Anglo-Saxon Protestants – the founders of the USA) in the media as in the Duke Lacrosse rape case. The Liberal DA in this case, with the real motivation of garnering the vote of blacks so that he can be reelected, only went silent when his victims fought back. US Liberals don't care how more sophisticated peoples around the world view this circus. It is confirmation of a lack of understanding of basic justice and it shows how primitive our society is at the same time as we tell the rest of the world how wonderful we are and tell them how they should behave. US Liberals feel that they are intellectually superior with jibes like 'when will Bush listen to the grown ups'. They are not intellectually superior but they are very Ugly.

David F. Evans, 23, of Bethesda, Md., a team captain who lived in the house where a black woman says she was sexually assaulted by three white players during a party, was charged with rape, first-degree sexual offense and kidnapping. Evans was indicted on the same charges as two of his teammates, Reade Seligmann, 20, of Essex Fells, N.J., and Collin Finnerty, 19, of Garden City, N.Y. All are privileged sons of privileged parents.

Evans graduated from Duke but did not attend the commencement ceremony. Before turning himself in he emphatically denied guilt at a news conference, becoming the first indicted player to speak publicly. "These allegations are lies and they will be proven wrong," he said. "Every member of the Duke University lacrosse team is innocent."

Evans said that he and his roommates had voluntarily helped the police when officers executed a search warrant at their house, and that he willingly provided DNA, spoke to investigators without a lawyer present and offered to take a polygraph test, which officials declined. He said that he and his lawyer, Joseph B. Cheshire V, had tried repeatedly but unsuccessfully to contact the district attorney, Michael B. Nifong, before his indictment. "As a result of his apparent lack of interest in my story, the true story," Evans said, he and his lawyer had arranged for a private polygraph test. "I passed it absolutely," he said, adding: "I've never had my character questioned before. Anyone who's met me knows that this didn't happen."

Evans was accompanied by his parents, Rae F. and David C. Evans, and by the seven other seniors on the lacrosse team, who stood behind him. Mrs. Evans, chairwoman of the Ladies Professional Golf Association board of directors and founder of the Evans Capitol Group, a Washington lobbying firm, wore on her suit lapel a large button with her son's photograph and jersey number. Her husband is a Washington lawyer. Their son graduated in 2002 from the Landon School, a private boy's preparatory school in Bethesda.

Evans's indictment came three days after defense lawyers received the results of a second round of DNA tests that they said failed to link any lacrosse players to the alleged crime. Tests on a fake fingernail found at the scene showed DNA from multiple sources and could not affirmatively exclude Evans, the lawyers said. "That, according to our expert, is about as weak a DNA analysis as you could ever have," The nail had been found in a trash can and could have been contaminated by used tissues or other items carrying the players' DNA.

Seligmann provided, through his lawyer, a detailed alibi including cash machine and food receipts that his lawyer says show that he could not have taken part in any assault.

A vaginal swab taken from the accuser showed semen from a male, named in the report on the results, who was not a Duke Lacrosse player. The test would not indicate when the semen was deposited.

The accuser, one of two strippers hired to perform at the party, said she had lost the nail during a struggle in which she was followed into the bathroom, attacked, raped and sodomized by three men. She later identified Seligmann and Finnerty in a photo lineup.

She also picked out Evans but was not certain of the identification. According to a transcript of her remarks during the lineup, the woman believed that Evans had been wearing a mustache at the time of the attack even though he had never had a mustache. It could be that he put on a false mustache as a clever disguise. Indeed there might now be a rash of crimes with people donning false mustaches.

The accuser is a stripper and multiple single mother. She retains her anonymity at the same time as the defendants' private lives are ruthlessly exposed. Feminists think that in sexual assault cases the presumption of innocence should not apply. The problem is that 9 percent of rape reports are dismissed even before charges are filed. Some women use the devastating charge of rape as a weapon. It is important to defend the interests of women as victims, but not to go so far as to accord women complaining of rape a presumption of honesty and objectivity.

The Culprit is Us

The United States is self indulgent and over indulgent in all its appetites. It leads the world in chronic obesity and with less than 5 percent of the world's population, consumes 25 percent of its oil, which is a non-renewable resource. How disgusting is that? The American public thinks "Me first and as much as I want even though everyone else will not have enough and they will not be able to afford what is left over after I have gorged myself. It would be easy for me to drive a more fuel efficient car and to drive less. But why should I – I am the self indulgent, self centered USA. Instead let's blame Bush. The increase in gasoline prices was within the control of the President."

China and India, with their fast-developing economies, still use far less energy than the United States, and it is unreasonable to expect them to maintain pre-industrial standards of living so that Americans can enjoy low oil prices.

Gasoline prices in the USA are in reality still very low particularly for a non-renewable resource. In Europe they are twice as high. The cost of gasoline is actually one of the lesser costs of driving a car and is a fraction of other costs of transportation such as air travel.

Life expectancy in the USA is lower than most developed countries because people over eat and over use their wheels. Higher priced gasoline would mean that they might eventually relearn to walk and then would live longer. Meanwhile they will blame Bush.

Harry Reid of Nevada, the Senate Democratic leader, proposed a two-month moratorium on collecting the federal gasoline tax, which would save motorists 18.4 cents a gallon. This money is needed for highway repairs. Gas hogs need to get the message that they must shed at least 1,000 pounds of vehicle girth to help the nation break its oil habit. We also need to reverse the budget deficit. We should increase gasoline prices to cover replacement costs.

An Ugly American

Senator Kerry used Vietnam as an opportunity to launch his political career, making good use of photo opportunities. He commanded his first swift boat in Vietnam, from December 1968 through January 1969. Kerry and crew operated without prudence in a Free Fire Zone, carelessly firing at targets of opportunity. His body count included-- a woman, her baby, a 12 year-old boy, an elderly man and several South Vietnamese soldiers. Kerry experienced his first combat action on Dec. 2, 1968. He was slightly wounded on his arm, earning his first Purple Heart. Kerry earned his second Purple Heart on Feb. 20, 1969 after sustaining minor shrapnel wound in his left thigh. On Feb. 28, 1969 after beaching his craft an enemy soldier sprang up from a hole not ten feet away and fled. The boat's machine gunner hit and wounded the fleeing Viet Cong as he darted behind a hooch. The gunner fired 50 rounds into the hooch before Kerry leaped from the boat and dashed in to administer the coup de grace to the seriously wounded Viet Cong. Kerry returned with a B-40 rocket and launcher. He was given a Silver Star for his actions. He also received a Purple Heart for a minor wound. On March 13, 1969, a mine detonated near Kerry's boat, slighting wounding Kerry in the right arm. He was awarded his third Purple Heart and a Bronze Star for valor. When later asked about the severity of the wounds, Kerry said that one of them cost him about two days of service, and that the other two did not interrupt his duty. After his third Purple Heart, Kerry requested to be sent home. Navy rules, he pointed out, allowed a thrice-wounded soldier to return to the United States immediately.

By the end of 1969, Kerry had become so inspired by anti-war beliefs that he petitioned to leave the Navy immediately so that he could run for Congress. Kerry received a discharge from the Navy six months early

As a national leader of Vietnam Veterans against War, Kerry campaigned against the effort of the United States to contain the spread of Communism. He used the blood of servicemen still in the field for his own political advancement by claiming that their blood was being shed unnecessarily. Under Kerry's leadership, VVAW members mocked the uniform of United States soldiers by wearing tattered fatigues marked with pro-communist graffiti. They dishonored America by marching in demonstrations under the flag of the Viet Cong enemy.

A Liberal is epitomized by John Kerry and his supporters. They are the fodder he pretends to champion. Massachusetts other senator, Ted Kennedy is another Liberal. Massachusetts has more than its fair share.

CHAPTER 5
UK AND USA

The Special Relationship

The USA pushed the UK into Europe. That was the end of the special relationship. To-day the UK is stuck somewhere between The European Union and an independent Island entity of decreasing importance saddled with its own declining recognition of the greatest Empire ever. At its height, Great Britain ruled a quarter of the world and the sun never set on the British Empire. To-day the British Empire is an embarrassing memory to Liberals.

Margaret Thatcher and Tony Blair are also subjected to Liberal hatred. Liberals are oblivious to the fact that Thatcher saved the UK from the disaster of socialism and that Blair in adopting the Thatcher mantle continued to save the country from being the sick man of Europe and gave Britons their current prosperity.

It is a mystery how Liberal pacifists can reconcile their views with the fact that the jack boot of Nazi Germany would now be on their pacifist necks if Britain had not declared war on Germany after leaving it almost too late.

Almost everyone in Germany was a Nazi from 1934 for about the next ten years until they started to suffer the awful consequences of their own behavior. When Germans express opinions, both they and we should remember that they initiated two world wars in the last century which caused terrible suffering and loss of life.

Britain has turned on the USA

The USA should no longer rely on Britain, which is no longer Great and is in the death throes of terminal Liberalism. Anti-Americanism and anti-Semitism have poisoned British politics. In a world of terrorism, the timing could not be worse for the UK.

Fury at Prime Minister Blair for being President Bush's poodle reached such a pitch that the only successful Labor prime minister ever was forced out of office because of his support for U.S. policy in Iraq and Israel. Labor's members of Parliament say his refusal to break with America by calling for an earlier cease-fire in Lebanon was the last straw. The disturbing fact is that Britain is consumed by a rampant anti-Americanism and an allied hostility toward Israel, which are driving public debate into irrationality, prejudice and appeasement.

In a Populus poll in The Times of London, 62% said the government should change its policy by distancing itself from the United States, being more critical of Israel and declaring a timetable for withdrawing from Iraq. A YouGov poll in The Spectator magazine revealed that while 53% wanted a tougher anti-terrorism policy, 45% wanted to be allied more closely with the Liberal European Union than with America. Only 14% supported closer US ties. As a result, the prospects for the alliance between Britain and the United States in the post-Blair era do not look promising. Despite being an instinctive Atlanticist and Thatcherite like Blair, Gordon Brown, the successor as Labor prime minister, is only a reluctant backer of US foreign policy, in consideration of his political survival.

Left-wing discourse is now staple fare on the BBC and applauded even by conservatively minded audiences in panel discussions, proclaims that the United States is the fount of Third World oppression and the greatest threat to world peace.

The British have traditionally believed with justification that Americans are vulgar upstarts who lack the gravitas that Britain has accrued from a thousand years of history. The new British, increasingly yobbish, are progressively junking that history. They are no longer proud of their Imperialist past, the British Empire or their finest hour. Schools no longer teach the history or values of the British nation on the grounds that national identity based on a majority culture is viewed as racist. Instead, they promote multiculturalism, the doctrine that minority values must have equal status to those of the majority. Loss of confidence in Britain's role in the world has demoralized its governing class so badly that it has come to believe that the nation state is the principal source of all ills from prejudice to war, and that legitimacy resides instead in supranational institutions. So no international action can be taken without sanctification by that holy of holies, the United Nations (the other 'superpower' who's role is to condemn and reign in the USA).

As a result, the British regard Bush's unilateral foreign policy with undiluted horror. This attitude is made worse by disdain for Bush himself, regarded unfairly by the Liberal media everywhere, starting in the USA, as a tongue-tied cowboy who actually believes in God — to the post-religious British, that is a certificate of lunacy.

A major cause of British anti-Americanism is Israel. Despite being the target for more than half a century of genocidal Arab and Muslim aggression, after Nazi Germany's attempt to annihilate the Jews had failed, Israel is widely perceived in Britain as the regional bully, and its acts of self-defense are viewed as the principal motor behind both the Middle East impasse and Islamic grievance because of its supposed refusal to allow the Palestinians to have a state of their own.

Thus John Denham, chairman of the parliamentary Home Affairs Select Committee, wrote that Israel's policies were making Britain a target for terror. America brought the 9/11 attacks upon itself, goes this type of thinking, because of its support for Israel — and the only reason Britain is now threatened by Islamic terror is because of Blair's support for the United States. So has opened a Pandora's box of anti-Jewish prejudice in Britain, all fueled by BBC misinformation and even more ghastly Liberal media sources such as The Guardian newspaper. Britons no longer know the facts – or care about the facts.

A recent report by the Parliamentary Committee Against Anti-Semitism found that since 2000, anti-Semitism is on the rise in Britain. It is now common to read in the news media, for example, that Jews are engaged in a global conspiracy that has subverted US foreign policy to serve the interests of Israel and put the rest of the world at risk. In April, for instance, The Independent newspaper illustrated an interview on the subject of the "Israel lobby" in America with a picture of the American flag in which the stars of the union were replaced with the Stars of David. The headline: "The United States of Israel." Thus the prejudice against America is inextricably conflated with prejudice against Jews and the Jewish state.

What is galling is that most US Jews are actually Liberal Democrats.

The dismaying truth is that, even after the suicide bombings in London, America's defense of the free world against Islamic terror is widely viewed in Britain as the cause of that terror. The paranoid bigotry that drives the jihad — that the United States and its Jewish puppet masters make up a giant conspiracy of evil — is being increasingly echoed within Britain's non-Muslim population.

Just as Britain stood alone in 1940, so does the USA to-day. The USA is also acrimoniously totally divided, with Liberals undermining the Administration wherever possible.

British View of America and Americans

Sixty-five percent of respondents consider Americans vulgar (Britain to-day is vulgar and so that response is a real insult); 72% think American society is unequal; 52% take a negative view of American culture; and 58% believe the U.S. is an essentially imperial power, one that wants to dominate the world by one means or another.

BBC coverage of Israel is very negative. Of 19 documentaries on Israel or the Palestinians aired by the BBC from 2000 to 2004, almost all were savagely critical of Israel. "The Accused" indicts Ariel Sharon as a war criminal; "Dead in the Water" alleges that Israel bombed an American ship in 1967 to disguise Israeli atrocities in the Sinai and to provoke an American nuclear strike on Cairo; and so on.

Compound this Liberal propaganda with the similar slant and tenor of nightly BBC coverage of Israel, the US, Iraq, Lebanon and Guantanamo Bay and it isn't hard to understand the sense of rage, easily descending to radicalism and violence, which typifies the political sensibilities of so many British Muslims.

The unemployment rate of British Muslims is three times that of the overall population. The country's Muslims tend not to participate in civic life but live on welfare in ghettoes. That is an incendiary mix.

Yet what really ought to terrify true Britons (those who can trace their British lineage and haven't emigrated) aren't the conclusions that divide mainstream and Muslim Britain, but the premises that unite them. These range from the credence given to people like Michael Moore and Noam Chomsky, to the antipathy for Tony Blair who is considered a lap dog of the USA, to the simplistic derision of the USA, anger over Iraq and the frenzied hatred of Israel.

Terrorism's roots in Britain are clear. What is extraordinary is how the Britain of 1940 in its finest hour has become the Britain of to-day.

The Differences between the USA and Britain

It is important to understand the different origins of Islamofascism. It was mainly Saudis who perpetrated 9/11. Pakistanis would now seem to pose the more insidious threat through immigration into the UK in particular.

One major difference between the United States and Britain is the United States' ideal of being a melting-pot meritocracy. Britain remains far more rigid, with less opportunity. In the United States, for example, Pakistani physicians are more likely to lead departments at hospitals or universities than they are in Britain. Throughout the USA, Pakistanis are prospering. Mean household income in the United States in 2002 was $57,852 annually, while that for Asian households, which includes Pakistanis, was $70,047. By contrast, about one-fifth of young British-born Muslims are jobless, and many subsist on welfare.

Only 500,000 people of Pakistani descent live in the United States, with some 35 percent in the New York metropolitan area. Chicago has 100,000; thousands of immigrants and their American-born offspring flock to Devon Avenue because of its restaurants and traditional goods, including wedding saris for women and long, elaborate shirts and gilded slippers for men. The avenue's half-dozen mosques are more conservative than elsewhere in Chicago, with the imams emphasizing an adherence to Muslim tradition but unlike Britain and Pakistan, they do not endorse using violence for political or religious aims.

We have to understand the tipping point that pushes angry young Muslim men to accept an ideology that endorses suicide and mass murder. We are talking about a cult mind-set and how a cult does its brainwashing.

Tariq Ramadan and Pseudo Intellectuals at Oxford University

Tariq Ramadan is a Swiss-born Muslim activist. The Department of Homeland Security revoked Ramadan's visa, preventing him from taking up a teaching post in the United States. But Oxford was proud to have him teaching there. "Isn't it better to be open to other people's points of view?"

The "point of view" of Tariq Ramadan, a grandson of Hassan al-Banna, the founder of the Muslim Brotherhood is their credo: "Allah is our objective. The Prophet is our leader. Qur'an is our law. Jihad is our way. Dying in the way of Allah is our highest hope." Is this what Ramadan, too, believes? That is not an easy question to answer. It is significant, we think, that he should deny that there is "any certain proof" that Osama bin Laden was involved in the terrorist attacks of 9/11. (If "there is no truth," who can object?) He is said to have met early and often with various members of al Qaeda and other Islamist groups. Ever sensitive to the nuances of language, he refers to such atrocities as the bombings in Bali and Madrid as "interventions." In truth, Ramadan is a consummately slippery customer—ferociously articulate, adept in deploying the rhetoric of compromise, tolerance, "dialogue," and accommodation. He is, as the French writer Caroline Fourest notes in her book Brother Tariq: The Doublespeak of Tariq Ramadan, a "master of the art of euphemism."

His approach, seemingly moderate, succeeds in attracting the more or less modern Muslims that he will gradually initiate into radicalism, and then fundamentalism, the environment that produces future terrorists. How? By pretending to advocate a form of fraternity and tolerance that has the effect, above all, of making any moderate Muslim feel guilty in comparison to the extremists. Once their vigilance has been dismantled, he has only to put those he has thus outfitted in touch with the Brothers' network.

In a 2005 article in Le Monde, for example, Ramadan called for a "moratorium" on the application of some aspects of Muslim law—e.g., stoning adulteresses to death, executing anyone who apostatizes from Islam, cutting off the hands of thieves, and other benevolent prescriptions brought to you by the "religion of peace." True, Ramadan then went on to criticize the West's "unilateral condemnations" of such practices, arguing that "Western governments and individuals have a major responsibility to allow the Muslim world to engage in this debate serenely within Islam's interior."

Now a "moratorium" is a temporary suspension of some activity or state of affairs. Should we be pleased that Ramadan wants his fellow Muslims to leave off stoning errant women until—when? Next Tuesday? After the New Year? Until Europe finally "goes Muslim" altogether and silly Western scruples like the prohibition against maiming criminals or protecting religious freedom can be dispensed with for good?

The dreaming spires of Oxford! "Tolerance" for folks like Tariq Ramadan is not enough, because one tolerates only that of which one disapproves. What Ramadan wants is "respect" and approbation, not tolerance. He wants us to embrace him and his beliefs—until they triumph to such an extent that he can reject us categorically in the name, not of tolerance or diversity, but of divine truth. "Everyone looks at the world from a different point of view. Tariq Ramadan's "point of view" is that of a cold-blooded Islamist who believes that Islam is the cure for the malaise wrought by Liberal values. His revision of the jihadist paradigm—peaceful but total—is brilliant in its way, and he may well turn out to be a major Islamist intellectual, far surpassing even his grandfather's influence. His cry of death to the West is a quieter and gentler jihad, but it's still jihad. There's no reason for Western Liberals to try to understand that point of view.

That gets to the nub of the issue—both with respect to the reality of Tariq Ramadan's agenda and what we in the West should think of it, which is to condemn it. That is not a popular "point of view" at Oxford. But then political realities have always had a difficult time surviving in that rarefied air. On the High Street last month we saw a church placard announcing that they were "praying" to be a more "inclusive" congregation. And remember the Oxford Union in 1933: "Resolved that we will in no circumstances fight for king and country." To have condemned Tariq Ramadan would have been to exhibit what Oxford Liberal intellectuals consider to be "cultural essentialism" and a lamentable tendency to demonize "the Other." How comical Tariq Ramadan and his friends must find these effete moral gymnastics. "An open mind is the best way to look at the world." It's such emollient advice, especially if you are bent on making sure that you alone will decide what counts as openness.

CHAPTER 6
HOW LIBERALS
THINK

The Liberal Point of View

After the fall of Saddam Hussein's regime, Americans were seen as the saviors of the oppressed peoples of Iraq. Now, our troops are seen as the occupying force, far from being liberators. Americans expressed appropriate outrage, and sadness, at the apparently senseless slaughter of two dozen Iraqi civilians in Haditha. But can we as easily absolve ourselves for the thousands of civilian deaths that were a predictable and inevitable outcome of our war of choice?

President Bush has demanded that young military personnel do something impossible and they are breaking under the strain. The world is watching us losing our good reputation.

Shouldn't our troops be taken out of harm's way immediately? There will be roadside bombs to infuriate them without end. They are only human. It is Vietnam in Iraq

Mistakes have been made, we have been misled, and the only people who have paid are the dead, the wounded and their loved ones.

What the Bush administration is saying is that we can't leave as long as the war can continue to be fought by other people's children. It is time to confront every one of the war's supporters, about the conversations that they have had with their own children concerning service in this war.

The war's sacrifice has not been shared equally by the children of the war's supporters. If the children of the well-to-do were sent to Iraq, the war would come to a quick end. We believe that if the military were made up of people of all classes, we wouldn't have gone to war in the first place. Bring back the draft. Only then we will choose our wars more carefully.

We must respect the lives of the women and men in the armed forces. What better way to respect their lives than to protect them by bringing them home? President Bush has not attended a single funeral. He has missed nearly 2,500 chances to show personal respect. It should be mandatory that each of the officials who flung us into this miserable war should be the ones to knock on the family door and deliver the bad news, accompany the family to the funeral, and write a personal letter on the occasion of each death. We understand that it is virtually impossible for us to know anything about the Iraqis who have been killed, but we don't understand why any American must remain anonymous. Every newspaper worth its salt should print the names of those who have been killed or wounded on the front page each day.

If we cannot, as a democratic nation, muster the forces necessary to fight a war, then it is clear that we should not be fighting that war. By not enlisting the people of the United States have spoken. Are mercenaries the inevitable next generation in warfare? Before we sanction corporate warfare, we need to ask ourselves if this is what America is all about. For centuries, good people of the world have engaged in a struggle to find a way in which all cultures can coexist peacefully. Let us not undo all this good work and go backward to the Middle Ages. If we as citizens are unwilling to volunteer to defend and protect our nation, the alternative of hiring mercenaries to provide security in Iraq as we are doing, is unacceptable. We must restore pride in our country and the policies it pursues so that the military will again be a calling aspired to by our young. To relegate an obligation of citizenship and patriotism to hired guns is heartbreaking.

We said that we would leave when Iraq became a sovereign nation and wanted us to leave. The sovereign government of Iraq says we are wantonly killing Iraqis and that it may hold our soldiers responsible under the Iraqi justice system — that we are, in effect, enemies of the Iraqi people.

Evidently, we've more than worn out our "welcome" in Iraq. It's time to go home, in spite of the mess we've made.

In his book, Senator Edward M. Kennedy writes that Bush's decision to invade Iraq was an example of preventive war — attacking a nation to prevent it from developing the ability to threaten the United States. He states that a similar manner of thinking led the Japanese to attack Pearl Harbor in 1941, since Japan was seeking to block the US military buildup in the Pacific. In his opinion, preventive war is consistent with neither our values nor our national security. It gives other nations an excuse to violate fundamental principles of civilized international behavior, and the downward spiral we initiate could well engulf the whole planet. He adds that war should always be our last resort. Instead, the Bush administration made preventive war an option of first resort.

On April 17th, 2006 the New York Times said that the invasion of Iraq was not about terror. It was about oil and schoolboy fantasies of empire and whatever weird oedipal dynamics were at work in the Bush family.

It is ironic that almost 50 years ago, Ted Kennedy's brother launched a clandestine invasion of Cuba. On April 17, 1961, about 1,500 CIA-trained Cuban exiles launched the disastrous Bay of Pigs invasion of Cuba in a failed attempt to overthrow the government of Fidel Castro. The Bay of Pigs Invasion was a United States-planned and funded landing by armed Cuban exiles in southwest Cuba in an attempt to overthrow the government of Fidel Castro and marked the climax of anti-Cuban US actions. US-Cuban tensions had grown since Castro had overthrown the regime of General Fulgencio Batista on January 1, 1959. The Kennedy administration had made the judgment that Castro's shift toward the Soviet Union could not be tolerated, and moved to overthrow him.

There is no similarity between Pearl Harbor and the forcible removal of Saddam Hussein. Kennedy is simply playing on US emotions by his link to this heinous attack by Japan, which finally persuaded the US belatedly to enter into the Second World War. A more accurate parallel is a comparison of Hitler and Saddam. None of the allies responded quickly enough against the threat of Hitler in a preventive or pre-emptive war. Eventually it was Britain and France which declared war on Germany and not the other way round. The USA still sat on the sidelines because of the Kennedy philosophy. Indeed Kennedy's father was a Nazi supporter and an admirer of Hitler!

As for Kennedy's assertion that the Bush administration made preventive war an option of first resort against Saddam, he has a conveniently short memory about Saddam initiating the eight year Iran war, genocide by Saddam in gassing Kurds, the 1991 Persian Gulf War when Saddam invaded Kuwait, Saddam's repeated disregard for UN Security resolutions, UN sanctions against Iraq and Saddam's obstruction of UN weapons experts which led to the whole world to believe that Saddam still had weapon's of mass destruction.

Kennedy's domestic proposals might be more acceptable in France and would hasten the economic decline of France.

Was Iraq liberated from Saddam Hussein or was Iraq invaded by the Bush Administration as our Liberals keep telling the world?

President Bush's approval rating in polls is 31%. His enemies consider him to be incompetent and arrogant. According to Liberals, his response to tragedy and adversity is to promote and flatter the incompetent and ignore the advice of cooler (Liberal) heads. He sold a war to the American people with lies and deceit. Now we must think of all the lives that have been lost, all those injured and the treasure spent.

Ordinary people are sweating it out to make ends meet with unaffordable gasoline prices, unaffordable health care, with concerns about an open-ended war in Iraq, the rising cost of living, the evaporating promise of Social Security and inequity in the income tax structure

He has run up a record deficit, kowtows to religious conservatives at every turn, ignores global warming and alienates many of America's longstanding allies. He mishandled preparations and the cleanup from Hurricane Katrina, demands for tougher border enforcement and skyrocketing energy prices.

Under Republican leadership, our country stands for military aggression, disdain for international cooperation, a presidency that is above the rule of law, and a host of policies that favor the very wealthy, widening the gap between haves and have-nots.

Freedom, to the G.O.P., means only the freedom of corporations to do whatever they want without paying their fair share of taxes.

And so Liberals go on. Their facts are wrong and their widely publicized views are destructive to the international standing and well being of the USA

Democratic Party

Democrats need look no further than the Pledge of Allegiance for their slogan and for the inspiration for their platform. Its last line is "with liberty and justice for all." Democrats should emphasize their belief in justice.

"We, the People of the United States, in Order to form a more perfect Union, establish Justice, insure domestic Tranquility, provide for the common defense, promote the general Welfare, and secure the Blessings of Liberty to ourselves and our Posterity, do ordain and establish this Constitution for the United States of America."

We must focus on the "common good," and reintroduce the New Deal. We will restore our national integrity as a guiding principle instead as a prelude to, the common good.

We will regain our national self-respect.

Key elements will be the right of choice for women, universal health and child care and educational opportunities. No American family should live in poverty.

In Iraq, we must withdraw by a stated date, with the participation of the United Nations. In the interim, Democrats will send in more troops in a spreading "inkblot" strategy to secure neighborhoods and deny support and safe haven for terrorists,

The fundamental difference between Liberals and Conservatives is whether one believes in collective responsibility or individual responsibility.

Concerns of Liberals –

"As a gay man in San Francisco, I have lost many friends and acquaintances to AIDS. I think it's important to note that the infection rate remains unacceptably high across the country, and that many people of all sexual preferences and of both sexes continue to pass away from AIDS-related conditions. The toll is not nearly as great as in the early 1980's to mid-1990's, but the numbers continue to rise. President Ronald Reagan did not even mention the word AIDS to the public until 1987. As one who lost 10 friends and acquaintances in one two-week period in the late 1980's, I will never forget the tardiness of our government's response. As one who supports gay marriage as an important response in the present age, I bemoan the continuing neglect."

"Liberalism is fundamentally about fairness and is evident in our country's greatest social and economic advances of the last century: a woman's right to vote, Social Security, access to college, and civil rights."

"People who have suffered depression and anxiety, self-treated perhaps with drugs and alcohol, and found themselves jobless, homeless, and at despair's door are not really employable. To suggest that they simply get a job robs them of the last vestige of dignity they might retain through the hope of a disability income and an opportunity to be housed."

"I am dissatisfied that we have made backward strides in education, healthcare, and the environment. I am dissatisfied the administration has isolated us from the world community and taken us down a road of endless war. I am dissatisfied we continue to turn our backs on the poor, the elderly, and the disabled."

Our Liberal Society

Catholic Charities of Boston announced that it was being forced to shut down its highly regarded adoption services, since it could not comply with the government's demand that it place children for adoption with homosexual couples since Catholic (and all Christian) teaching regards such adoptions as gravely immoral. There is no ambivalence in the Gospels. Homosexuality is a sin and sodomy is a lewd perversion contrary to nature. It has also given us the scourge of AIDS.

The Human Rights Campaign, one of the nation's largest homosexual political organizations, is driving this political agenda. Catholic Charities excels at arranging adoptions for children in foster care, particularly those who are older or handicapped, or who bear the scars of abuse or addiction. Yet the Human Rights Campaign and its Liberal allies would rather see this invaluable work come to an end than allow Catholic Charities to decline homosexual adoptions.

Catholic Charities made no effort to block same-sex couples from adopting. It asked no one to endorse its belief that homosexual adoption is wrong. It wanted only to go on finding loving parents for troubled children, without having to place any of those children in homes it deemed unsuitable. Homosexual couples seeking to adopt would have remained free to do so through any other agency

Will more states force religious organizations to swallow their principles as Massachusetts has done? Homosexual marriage proponents use the language of openness, tolerance, and diversity and yet every person and every religion that disagrees with them will be labeled as bigoted and openly discriminated against. Religious institutions will be hit with lawsuits if they refuse to compromise their principles.

When word spread at Harvard Law School that one of the most successful recruiters of its graduates, Ropes & Gray, was helping Catholic Charities explore ways to prevent same-sex couples from adopting children, the Homosexual organization, Lambda 'persuaded' Ropes to cease doing further work, by threatening protests, boycotts and picketing of Rope's recruiting efforts. Ropes are very concerned about public relations and were blackmailed into abandoning their principles not to discriminate against clients.

There is a Ropes Gray Room on campus. Ropes have done pro bono work for Homosexuals examining international trends supporting civil marriage for same-sex couples. The firm extends health benefits to domestic partners, and its anti-discrimination policy protects homosexual, lesbian, and bisexual employees.

The public policy issue is not whether Catholic Charities is correct about the harmfulness of same-sex parenting; it is whether an agency with by all accounts a highly successful record of adoption placement is to be prevented by over-regulation from exercising its best judgment about which families are suitable..

The church should not be forced to choose between the good of providing for children and the evil of placing them in inappropriate living situations. One could say that for the sake of the 1 in 5,000 adoptions in which Catholic Charities placed children with homosexuals, the Commonwealth has forced the church to end its century-old work of matching unwanted children with welcoming homes.

Catholic Charities and the bishops are not exempt from criticism. Their decision not to fight this unjust law is a blow to religious freedom in Massachusetts. Instead of just seeking a legislative or executive exemption, they should have directly challenged the constitutionality of the law. Unfortunately, the entanglement of religious charitable efforts with government funds led directly to this outcome. The church's teachings are not arbitrary impositions from Rome, but rather the expression of the requirements of the Gospel. No one should be surprised by them because they have been the consistent belief of the church for millennia. It is the Commonwealth of Massachusetts that has invented new and arbitrary doctrines.

The Church is not against a loving, committed relationship of same sex couples. As Saint Paul clearly stated and as the Church has always upheld sodomy is a sin. Sodomy has given the scourge of AIDS. Sodomy is deviate behavior and is normally associated with extreme promiscuousness and frequently with homosexual abuse of children

The Catholic Church has the strength of character to stand up for its beliefs. The prestigious firm of Ropes & Gray dropped Catholic Charities as a client because of pressure from the homosexual group at Harvard. This is happening at every level of government and in the private sector.

The Catholic Church welcomes homosexual members, but it does not recognize same-sex couples as part of God's plan for procreation. Whether the church is right or wrong on these issues, it is to be respected for not caving in to pressure from the secular world.

No one is forced to use a religious adoption agency. There are many other options available to them. Politicians are using this conflict to get votes, and special-interest groups are using it to further their agenda. The Catholic Church is merely staying true to itself.

To expose children wholesale to homosexual parenting in the name of human rights and tolerance seems a premature decision, especially since social science research on the issue is relatively limited. The question should be less about whether same-sex couples are loving, good people and more about what is best for children. Parenting, after all, is not just about parents.

For the Homosexual organization, Lambda to take a position that opposing viewpoints don't deserve representation should make us all extremely worried about the quality and ethics of these lawyers of tomorrow. Is this what they're teaching at Harvard Law? If the students in Lambda had any confidence in their position, they would join the debate, not suppress it. They, like Ropes & Gray, have demonstrated their cowardice.

Liberals Blame Haditha on George Bush

This Iraqi equivalent of My Lai is reverberated throughout the world; all one has to do was examine the Muslim and Arab reaction in the foreign press. American soldiers were seen as uniformed death squads no different from Saddam Hussein's Fedayeen.

Liberal arguments are as follows -

"What leads a marine to commit crimes on the scale of Haditha? The line of responsibility runs to one place: the highest office in the nation.

What makes these young soldiers so impervious to their abhorrent conduct? They are snatched from their ordinary lives, given comprehensive but not fully adequate training, taught to fight and kill and are then sent to war in a foreign country where they are mistrusted and hated. The constant roadside bombings, feeling hopeless and helpless, and seeing so much death around them of their friends and comrades, they reach the point where they just vent their frustrations and stress. They feel as well as know the hatred and anger toward them by a country that really did not want this gratuitous war in the first place.

Unless we demonstrate that we live by our own rules — the values and ethics that made this country uniquely admired throughout the world and that make it possible to win moral arguments — we are going to be defeated by the Islamic fascists, for they will have exposed us to the rest of the world as hypocrites. That was the real objective behind 9/11; not to "terrorize" us into submission. Osama bin Laden, Al Qaeda, North Korea, Iran and their ilk, either individually or collectively, cannot defeat America — only America can defeat America.

President Bush's legacy will be, in baseball terms, "Three strikes and you're out!" The wars — against the Taliban, Al Qaeda and Iraq— have in common premature claims of victory and the fact that, years later, they persist with mounting costs in lives, treasure and national reputation. By diverting resources to Iraq, Bush failed to secure his victories in Afghanistan. The Taliban are resurging; Osama bin Laden eluded capture; and the Iraqi invasion revitalized a decentralized terrorist network.

There is no foreseeable end to the war on terror. Nor to the Iraq war.

Are Bush and his inner circle considering a fourth war in the hope that a strike against Iran's nuclear facilities will somehow rally support to a flag-wrapped president sinking in the polls?"

More Liberal Sniping

The demise of Abu Musab al-Zarqawi was yet another feel-good moment in the war, like the toppling of the statue of Saddam Hussein, President Bush's "Mission Accomplished" speech in May 2003, the capture of Saddam Hussein, the restoration of Iraqi sovereignty, the first democratic elections in January 2005, and the agreement on a new constitution in October 2005. The emotions of these feel-good moments fade quickly, and we are forced to confront once again the cold reality of being stuck in an ineptly executed and protracted war based on false premises, with no postwar or exit strategy.

The real turning point in the Iraqi quagmire will come not with the death of one overrated terrorist who represented only a small percentage of the insurgents in Iraq, but with an effective Iraqi government that can exercise real authority and control beyond the Green Zone and with real policy changes on the part of the Bush administration.

When the United States government in all its might cannot even arrange for an orderly trial for Saddam Hussein, should we interpret the death of Abu Musab al-Zarqawi in a raid as a success, because a terrorist is dead? Or is it a failure, because the United States did not dare risk capturing him and having another embarrassing "showcase" trial that does not go forward?

People turned against this war because we were immorally lied into it, it was recklessly pursued at the expense of countless lives, and it was entered for political, perhaps even personal, reasons. None of those factors have changed with Mr. Zarqawi's death.

Does the Bush administration honestly believe that displaying gigantic framed photographs of one bloodied, dead terrorist, while prohibiting the photographing of thousands of flag-draped coffins returning with our war dead, will confuse the American public as to the real outcome of this calamitous misstep in American policy?

Many off us are familiar with the financial concept of leveraging ``other people's money" for one's personal advantage. Thanks to the Bush administration, we now have a variant: other people's children.

Those who joined to serve our country in the full- or part-time military, often enticed by offers of training or educational or health benefits, now often find that they cannot leave. Such enticements appeal only to those who suffer the misfortune of not having access to a trust fund or large parental bank account. As a result, the Bush administration's misbegotten war of choice is disproportionately fought by the sons and daughters of working or poor people to whom the estate tax would apply only if you aggregate the assets of everyone they know. The administration knows that any movement to place the progeny of the gilded class in jeopardy of falling into Iraq's insatiable grinder will result in a quick end to its dirty war.

More Liberal Wailing

Abu Musab al-Zarqawi, Al Qaeda's leader in Iraq, delighted in the slaughter of innocents, taking his hatred so far as to behead hostages personally. al-Zarqawi was a ruthless terrorist who initiated an orgy of death and destruction and was intent on slaughtering Muslims and non-Muslims alike, stoking the embers of hostility and enmity between Shiites and Sunnis and creating a climate of intimidation through the victimization of innocent peoples and the dismemberment of Iraq.

When al-Zarqawi was killed by the US military, The Liberal response was as follows –

"It is to be hoped that Abu Musab al-Zarqawi's death will result in the saving of American and Iraqi lives. But the reported euphoria is unbecoming. It is reminiscent of the television footage of Iraqis celebrating the deaths of American soldiers.

Abu Musab al-Zarqawi may have been killed, but there are many people to take his place as a terrorist leader. The insurgents might not have a clear purpose, but they are certainly clear about their animosity toward American troops. Our presence is galvanizing the insurgency.

Evil contains the seeds of its own destruction. Those who lie, torture and kill eventually become entrapped by their own sins. These are the sins of the Bush administration that have entrapped us in an ever more horrifying and brutal war.

Our society, with all its honesty, virtue and decency, began this war for immoral reasons. Where is there any leadership in this country that can present a case to the American people concerning the madness in Iraq?

It is so clear that our violence in Iraq is destroying our reputation in the world as a bastion of freedom and is creating a feeding frenzy for those who would like nothing more than to present Americans, all Americans, as the true focus of evil in the world. Have we as a people lost our senses? Where is the outrage? Is this war a reflection of our national morality? Taking out Abu Musab al-Zarqawi will only fuel more violence. Where does it end? The Bush administration has no answers.

We have brought carnage to Iraq by launching an ill-considered war that is being fought with other people's blood and with resources borrowed from future generations while the children of the elite go unscathed. But in considering what to do now, we cannot simply cut and run. The fact is that this war was authorized by Congress and begun by a president whose actions were ratified by the American electorate in 2004. The American people, including the apathetic that chose not to vote, are responsible for inflicting mayhem upon the people of Iraq, who had no vote on whether an invasion of their country was worth the horrible price.

Simply put, this mess is our fault, and we cannot walk away from it and leave Iraq in anarchy. We should institute a draft and clean things up with the blood of everyone, rich and poor.

Our nation is in deep denial with respect to Iraq, but there is an additional explanation for our country's indifference. The average American is preoccupied with other concerns, including making ends meet, job insecurity, trying to attend to each other's and the children's needs when both partners work, contending with congested roads, inadequate public transportation and long commutes to work that reduce family time. Most people are so stressed out that Iraq takes a back seat to these concerns. While this is unfortunate, it is understandable."

More Liberal Blackmail

In the five years that George Bush has been president, the Food and Drug Administration has been led by a confirmed commissioner for just one year. Senate Democrats have refused to confirm a leader for the agency as long as it refuses to allow over-the-counter sales of a morning-after contraceptive, which has been for sale by prescription since 1999. These pills are 89 percent effective if taken within 72 hours. Liberals want the convenience and anonymity of over-the-counter sales for those who indulge in casual unprotected sex and who do not want to involve a doctor – or parent. Another two women have just died after taking this pill, making seven since 2000, but that is not enough to influence the Liberal agenda of free sex with anonymity. Once again the Liberals make us all suffer for some trivial entitlement for the irresponsible sex junkies.

The FDA has been at the center of controversies concerning how it approves drugs before they go on the market and monitors problems that arise afterwards. The agency badly needs the direction that a confirmed commissioner could provide.

The General Public should not pay for people to indulge themselves whether it be preventable conditions like unwanted pregnancies or preventable illnesses. People who maintain their weight subsidize those who do not. Nonsmokers subsidize smokers. According to the Centers for Disease Control, in 1991 there were 49 states that had fewer than 15 percent of their citizens overweight. In 2000, there was only one such state (Colorado). This obesity epidemic and the resulting high-cost medical conditions are caused entirely by preventable factors, such as diet and lifestyle. Similarly, smoking is associated with many high-cost forms of illness. The Liberal entitlement mentality prevents real solutions to these problems. They do exist if the sacred cow of freedom for the individual is subordinated to responsible behavior by the individual.

When the FDA does not fulfill its obligations adequately, our litigious society has an orgy subsequently when drugs have unwanted and unforeseen harmful side effects. The consequence is higher priced and fewer new drugs.

Despite all, George Bush has attempted to accommodate Liberals. Since he took office, government spending has increased by more than 25 percent, the largest increase under any president since Democrat Lyndon B. Johnson. President Bush and the Republican Congress dramatically increased the government's role in, and overall spending on, education and Medicare by enacting the No Child Left Behind law and the new prescription drug entitlement for seniors. The President took these actions in a genuine attempt for bipartisan cooperation. Now the party is over. Conservative voters want swift congressional action to secure the border and enforce immigrations laws, tax cuts, and a constitutional amendment outlawing same-sex marriage, new abortion restrictions, and measures to restrain government spending.

CHAPTER 7
ADDLED LIBERAL
THINKING

Liberals are Losers.

The response to the UK plot to blow planes out of sky and the arrest of British Muslims has been for Moderate British Muslim Leaders to call for special bank holidays to mark their religious festivals and the introduction of Sharia Law. They have demanded that Tony Blair changes foreign policy to favor Islam. Terrorist Imams have been spewing their hate in UK Mosques since the 1990s and now more than ever UK authorities are desperately trying not to offend Muslims. The passport photograph of a five year old girl was rejected by the UK Passport Office because she was wearing a sleeveless dress.

The situation is essentially no better in the rest of Europe. The genie is out of the bottle. There are now too many Islamofascists for any means of painless resolution.

Religious freedom was an important right when people were being persecuted for their religious beliefs. As an example the protection of the Amish in the USA and their responsible citizenship has been laudable. To the contrary, Islam is being used to persecute people who have other religious beliefs, not only in Muslim countries but also in the West. We need a different response to their behavior. Diplomacy is not the way and we cannot negotiate with terrorists. We are also running out of time as the war on terror is increasingly unacceptable to Liberals in Europe. Military body bags are now as ill received in Europe as they are in the USA and relatively low civilian casualties are treated as catastrophic. We hand terrorists a victory every time there is any publicity as everything is now played out in the full glare of the Liberal media. In increasingly antiwar America, similar dynamics are at work.

One twisted Liberal argument is that the USA brutalizes Muslims, which in turn foments Islamist terror. In fact jihadists have never needed foreign policy grievances to justify their violence. There was no equivalent to the Iraq police action in 1993, when Islamists first tried to blow up the World Trade Center, or in 2000, when they attacked the American destroyer Cole. Indeed, that assault took place after United States-led military intervention saved thousands of Muslims in Bosnia and Kosovo.

Most Muslims die at the hands of other Muslims. In Sudan, black Muslims are starved, raped, enslaved and slaughtered by Arab militias, with the consent of an Islamic government. Where is the Muslim fury against genocide? In Pakistan, Sunnis hunt down Shiites every day just as they are doing in Iraq. Islam is not a religion of peace.

We need to deal with Islamofascism in the West in the same way that Britain handled Nazis at the end of World War 2. The British found that German prisoners could be divided into three groups. 10% were hard core Nazis. 10% were capable of being ethical leaders. The other 80% followed the leadership of whoever was in charge. Britain isolated the 10% hard core Nazis and the other 90% became responsible world citizens. The West's weak kneed Liberals need to accept that we must profile, hunt down and imprison the Islamofascists in our midst before they contaminate the vast majority of Muslims who, seemingly, do not think for themselves.

Because we have more sensible (when it is done legally) immigration into the USA of better educated Muslims and because Immigrants Pledge Allegiance when they become citizens (and mean it), we are better off, but we need to adopt tough love in the USA without delay for all US residents if we are not to become a basket case like Europe.

Partisan US Politics

U.S. Sen. Joe Lieberman has been rejected by fellow Democrats for supporting the overthrow of Saddam Hussein and continuing to support President Bush in his war against Terrorism. He will now stand as an Independent and accused his Democratic opponents of not fully understanding the danger facing the nation. He also reiterated his disgust for political partisanship when it comes to national security. "We are at war with a brutal enemy," Lieberman said. "How the heck can we be in a battle in which we are fighting as Democrats and Republicans against each other when these terrorists certainly don't distinguish based on party affiliation? They want to kill any and all of us. I'm not saying we shouldn't have healthy disagreement and discussions about national security, but to make it into a partisan political football is just unacceptable and in my opinion un-American. I'm worried that too many people, both in politics and out, don't appreciate the seriousness of the threat to American security and the evil of the enemy that faces us -- more evil or as evil as Nazism and probably more dangerous than the Soviet Communists we fought during the long Cold War."

Lieberman said Democrats' plan to withdraw troops from Iraq will only embolden the terrorists and put the U.S. at risk. "If we say we will get out by a date certain, it will be taken as a tremendous victory by the same people who wanted to blow up these planes in this plot hatched in England. It will strengthen them and they will strike again."

We do have a Plan for our Military to leave Iraq. It is important that this information is not leaked. The Liberal media, the New York Times in particular and Liberals in general should only be told when we want our enemies to know.

Liberal Academics

Many Liberal Academics are woolly minded terrorist sympathizers who believe the worst about the United States and the best about its enemies. The University of Wisconsin at Madison is teaching that the Sept. 11, 2001, attacks on the World Trade Center and the Pentagon were plotted by the US government to create an excuse for war. It is part of a course on "Islam: Religion and Culture." Defenders of the course say that academic freedom is at stake and so the course content should not be censored.

Mir Babar Basir, a recent University of Wisconsin graduate and former president of the Muslim Students Association, says that this viewpoint has many supporters.

Denying the link between Islamic fanaticism and Sept. 11 is not helping the acceptance of moderate Muslims in the West.

Liberals have zero tolerance for anyone who supported military action. Senator John McCain, Republican of Arizona, talking about Senator Joseph I. Lieberman, Democrat of Connecticut who supported the Iraq police action to depose Saddam Hussein, remarked "I hesitate to say anything nice about him for fear that it would be used against him. And that's a terrible commentary on the state of politics and the political climate today."

The Age of Impunity

Sudan's leaders sent out a letter last week warning governments against volunteering their troops for a United Nations peacekeeping force for Darfur. US Liberals nevertheless are pressuring the Bush Administration to invade the Sudan. Once US troops are there and a quagmire develops, they will change their tune as they always do.

The New York Times points out the impotence of the USA in an Editorial they call the Age of Impunity. They point to Iran, which is still defiantly enriching uranium. And the North Koreans, who blew off the rest of the world when they blew off what they said was a nuclear weapon this week.

They add that it wasn't supposed to be this way. "The Iraq war and President Bush's with-us-or-against-us war on terrorism was supposed to frighten the bad guys so much that they wouldn't dare cross the United States. But the opposite has happened. President Bush has squandered so much of America's moral authority that efforts to shame or bully the right behavior from adversaries (and allies) sound hollow. Ethnic cleansing has already left more than 200,000 dead and displaced more than two million in Darfur. The New York Times simplistically states that closing our eyes for another two years isn't an answer. Washington needs to assert its leadership, no matter how tattered."

The tragedy of Darfur is a consequence of Liberal ambivalence and has nothing to do with moral authority. It does have a great deal to do with Liberal arrogance, self-righteousness and playing the blame game over Iraq. No US Administration will put itself in the dock again to be undermined and pilloried by US Liberals after taking agreed military action, with its inevitable unforeseen consequences.

US Liberals are so blinded by their own sense of moral superiority that they do not realize that they are alone in their view. No country in the world looks on the US as being morally superior and it has nothing to do with George Bush having squandered America's moral authority. In much of the world we are seen as the great decadent Satan corrupting the rest of the world socially and culturally.

The Germans considered themselves to be the Master Race. The North Koreans have the same delusion. North Korea's Kim Jong-il is one stage worse than Saddam Hussein and he poses a different kind of threat. He is less likely to be a direct threat to his neighbors, but he is more likely to sell nuclear weapons to terrorists. Since he is less predictable and on China's doorstep, he is also more difficult to deal with

Liberal Arrogance

What if liberal democracies have now evolved to a point where they can no longer wage war effectively because they have achieved a level of humanitarian concern for others that dwarfs any really cold-eyed pursuit of their own national interests? Can it be that the moral greatness of our civilization -- its astonishing focus on the value of the individual above all -- is endangering the future of our civilization as well?

What if the Allies during World War II had been confronted daily both with reports of Allied casualties and with images of dead and wounded German civilians, including children and old people? What if public opinion had been as troubled by casualties as we are today? Would there still be a free world to speak of?"

Pelosi acknowledges that both Saddam Hussein in Iraq and Hafez al-Assad in Syria, quelled uprisings by wiping out thousands, committing genocide Nevertheless she could not bring herself to admit that it was morally right to depose Saddam Hussein. She ends with the lame comment that "If fear makes us squander our moral progress, it will be a tragic paradox indeed."

Liberal arrogance trumps logical thought.

Liberal Decadence

Liberals blinded by their enmity towards George Bush state that it is his actions in Afghanistan, Iraq and Lebanon that have radicalized Muslims. According to them he is the cause of Terrorism. They never make a positive suggestion but favor appeasement and a permissive response to the problems of Islam. European Liberals and many in the USA would abandon Israel. Liberals would like a war where no one was killed.

The real issue is one of incompatible cultures between the Muslim world and the West -

In a park in central Berlin, naked males sit on the grass stroking their rampant genitals to attract a homosexual partner. After sodomizing each other, they repeat the procedure. In shop windows in the red light district in Amsterdam, female meat is on display. At the ornate Galleries Lafayette in Paris, shapeless black shrouded figures stand in line on Prada shoes to buy Chanel. The black brooding presence is also strong in London's Oxford Street, mingling with bejeweled belly buttons of English teenagers. Ironically, Leicester is the counterfeiting capital of Europe where British Pakistanis finance terrorism by providing fake Chanel and Prada to the woman in the street.

On the plane to Saudi Arabia, the designer clothes are replaced by burkas and women then walk dutifully two paces in arrears. The religious police are ready to stop any Western behavior.

The West showed Saudis how to get black gold out of the ground. Arabs consider manual work to be demeaning and so Asians become temporary residents to provide labor, but they have to be shipped out when they die as dead Infidels cannot remain in the Kingdom.

The USA was a melting pot of different cultures. Immigrants had to work hard to survive. In the UK, the welfare state welcomes Muslims with free hand outs, free housing and without the need to work. They are resented and despised. Enoch Powell is being proven right. In Europe there is no melting pot. There is a powder keg.

The news of a second, more devastating 9/11-like terror plot uncovered by the British authorities underscores starkly the facile nature of the incessant lambasting of the Bush administration recently for its pursuing clear-eyed, tough-minded measures to protect the United States from just such an attack. In light of the intended magnitude of the thwarted attack — "mass murder on an unimaginable scale," as one London official described it — the out-of-touch-with-reality critics of President Bush come off looking more benighted than ever.

Rather than trying constantly to undermine the efforts of a wartime president to keep us safe, Liberals should redirect their outrage at the terrorists the world over who would like nothing better than to kill every man, woman and child who does not share their radical, religious fundamentalist worldview.

Liberal Obfuscation

There are only 2.3 million members remaining in the Episcopal Church as most have found it to be a Liberal Club with cafeteria beliefs based on individual values and not on New Testament teachings. The vast majority of the 90 million Anglicans worldwide is appalled at the callous disregard of the Anglican Church's position on homosexuality, that the Episcopal Church agreed to and then chose to ignore. Liberal Episcopalians think with typical US arrogance that they know what is best, since they believe they are intellectually superior to the vast majority who happen to be young Asians and Africans. The Episcopal Church is now splitting apart and so far six dioceses have become independent because they could not live with a church that defiantly elects an openly homosexual bishop and that encourages same-sex marriage.

St. Luke's in Darien, Connecticut is more vibrant than most Episcopal parishes and has 3,000 members. Most of them are very well heeled and rely on the church for some sort of moral compass in a society where permissive upbringing of children is commonplace. Most members have casual beliefs and a matching casual church attendance. There is no requirement to believe anything that Christ taught other than to love and accept others and to be non-judgmental of others. Based on this belief system, permissive sodomy is OK and practicing homosexuals can become Church leaders. Like most Liberal positions the problem is that by definition it is not possible to draw a line under what is acceptable and what is not. New Testament teachings are clear. Liberal positions are variable and elastic.

The Archbishop of Canterbury, the spiritual leader of the Anglican Communion, faced with a worldwide schism because of the unilateral arrogance of the Episcopal Church in ignoring agreed Church teachings, has asked all 38 regional churches in the Communion to agree to a covenant that would limit each church's autonomy and so prevent further Episcopal destructive unilateralism. Those that do not agree would be given second-tier status in the Communion.

Self-styled Father (he should read what the Bible says) Anderson at St. Luke's has held feel good meetings on the situation. His obfuscation of the real issue, like all Liberal Church Leaders, is troubling. It is clear that his parishioners are in the dark about Christianity and Church teachings on homosexuality. The following is an exchange at one of his meetings.

"So in other words," Martha Cook, a university professor and member of the vestry at St. Luke's said, "the conservatives could literally take over our rightful spot in the Communion, and the majority of the American church would be on the outs?"

(It is not a question of being conservative; it is a question of following what the Church interprets as Christian teaching. Individual interpretation by definition means that there is no Episcopal Church which is just about what has happened).

"The vast majority of the Episcopal Church would be considered the 'off brand,' " Father Anderson said.

(Most Episcopal clergy are Liberals with an Agenda that is not to teach what Christ and his Apostles said. Contrast the Episcopal Church with what the Pope says. He and his advisors continue to preach the Gospels.)

"The vast majority of parishes are somewhere in the middle, with members on each side of the debate who feel connected to the Episcopal Church and to Anglican tradition, said the Rev. William Sachs, "What's really going on in the pews of Episcopal churches is they don't necessarily want to align with either side," he said. "They want to get on with life. They want this thing resolved."

(This obfuscation of the issue is outrageous; Christ taught that he who is without sin should cast the first stone. That is not the issue. The Episcopal Church leadership unilaterally, in defiance of an agreement with fellow Anglicans worldwide and without even consulting the people in the pews, elected a self proclaimed sodomist, who does not even believe the Apostle's Creed, to be Bishop, even though they knew his election would be unacceptable to the Anglican Community. They clearly have an Agenda which has nothing to do with Christianity).

Some said they were shocked because the Archbishop's statement came just six days after the Episcopal Church convention passed a resolution intended to mend fences with the Anglican Communion. The Archbishop's statement raised the prospect of "ordered and mutually respectful separation" between churches that could not come to agreement, suggesting to many Episcopalians that they would eventually have to choose sides.

(How dishonest! The Episcopal Church convention was defiant and elected a female leader who supports homosexual leadership knowing that it would cause further angst).

"It used to be Communion über alles," said Judy Holding, a student at Yale Divinity School and a chaplain at Greenwich Hospital, "but now I'm asking, at what price Communion?" Ms. Holding said later: "At a certain point for me, it's not worth the price. I would not sign that covenant if it means we have to compromise Christian love and social justice."

(Judy Holding makes no mention and neither does anyone else of Christian teaching. Since she has regaled us with her credentials, perhaps she could explain why Christian love and social justice are better than other kinds. She would be more credible if she was a chaplain in Calcutta. Judy Holding's reference to social justice presumably is because she thinks that homosexuals are not being justly treated. Does she have concern for the innocent victims of the scourge of AIDS spread by homosexual men and now being transmitted to babies of bisexual, promiscuous men, and young girls violated in the belief that they will cure men with AIDS? Does she have concern for the many, many Anglicans who have left the Episcopal Church because of the Liberal Agenda replacing Christian faith?)

Father Anderson asked how many in the room had even heard of the Anglican Communion before 2003, when Anglican archbishops in places like Nigeria and Uganda began protesting the election of an openly homosexual bishop in New Hampshire. Only a third of the 30 parishioners in the room raised their hands.

(It is nothing to be proud of to admit that you have taught nothing of the Church to which you profess to belong. Also don't obfuscate. The Liberal cabal in places like Darien elected Robinson knowing of the opposition of Anglican Archbishops in Nigeria, Uganda and most other parts of the world. You might think you are superior but you are not).

David Kelley, whose parents were also St. Luke's members, told the gathering, "All this business of consulting with other churches in the Communion, I'm not aware of the African churches consulting with us."

(I will blame this ignorant response on your church leadership. Next time African churches behave unilaterally, will be the first).

Father Anderson closed the gathering with a brief sketch of Anglican history. Queen Elizabeth I gave the church the Book of Common Prayer, he told them, and the church came to be distinguished by its flexibility. "We've never been bound by common belief, but by common prayer," he said. "Anglicans have always had a generous openness. I just feel that now there's a cold wind blowing. As someone here said tonight, it feels un-Anglican to me."

(So called flexibility and cafeteria beliefs are a modern invention of Liberal Episcopalians so that they can believe what they want and behave as they want. Instead of rewriting history, I suggest you learn of the true origins of the Church of England. You would have been drawn and quartered as a heretic.)

Now we know why the rest of the world thinks of us as Ugly Americans.

A pious gathering is not needed to resolve this issue. All that it would take is for Gene Robinson to resign. How any true Christian could destroy the Church to push homosexuality as an alternative lifestyle against the wishes of the vast majority of church members worldwide, is difficult to comprehend. Robinson would do well to read the New Testament about causing people to lose their faith.

European Liberal Claptrap

The European Union ensures continual kidnappings and beheadings since they make the fatal mistake of negotiating with terrorists and give full media coverage. True to form, the European Union issued a thundering denunciation saying it was shocked and dismayed by Israeli air strikes in Lebanon, following an errant Israeli missile which went off course. They stated that there is no justification for attacks causing casualties among innocent civilians, most of them women and children.

Europeans have effectively endorsed the benefit of using human shields when terrorists launch missiles randomly to kill Israelis. Israelis have the technology to seek out these missile sites but the European condemnation of Israel encourages Hezbollah to use more human shields to prevent an Israeli response.

Just as appeasement of the Nazis ensured their success, this appeasement of both Hamas and Hezbollah will ensure their success.

Terrorists deliberately target civilians indiscriminately and so the statement and implicit policy and actions of the European Union will ensure many more deaths of civilians on a continuing and increasing basis. That the deaths of 50 women and children, who were kinfolk of terrorists, could generate such an emotional outcry makes such deaths a most valuable currency for terrorists who are delighted to kill women and children. The response in any case lacks any sense of proportion. When US troops finally released the surviving skeletons from European concentration camps, six million had been killed. Almost all of these were Jews. Is that still the essential difference for Europeans? Are Israelis not innocent civilians whereas Lebanese Shiites are?

All moral people grieve over the loss of innocent civilian lives. But the finger of blame was pointed in the wrong direction. Missiles have been fired by Hezbollah from Qana at Israeli cities and citizens. Before air attacks, Israel warned Lebanese citizens to leave their towns and villages. Hezbollah used a civilian center as a staging ground for military aggression. It is Israel's right to defend its citizens against missile attacks. Hezbollah bears full responsibility for the tragic loss of life in Qana.

Israel apologized for the air strikes and expressed sorrow that civilians were killed. Hezbollah and Hamas will never apologize for all of the civilians killed in rocket attacks or children murdered when school buses were bombed in past years.

Israel opened safe corridors across Lebanon to allow non-combatants to leave and for shipments of medical aid and food. Hezbollah guerrillas blocked them to create a humanitarian crisis, for which Israel was blamed.

The Fault Lines in Liberal Societies

With tensions rising between Muslim immigrants, their children and the native-born populations in Western Europe, the question of how to integrate foreigners has stirred passions across the continent. Germany, like the Netherlands, France and Belgium, has a large Muslim population clinging to the language and traditions of their home countries.

Unemployment is rampant both among immigrants and native-born Germans, and violence is endemic in schools with large immigrant student bodies. Germany is home to 3 million Muslim immigrants. The majority were invited to the country as guest workers, mainly from Turkey. Faced with a labor shortage in the 1950s, and 60s, West

Germany encouraged foreigners to fill positions in factories and in construction.

The Germans recruited untrained and uneducated people. It was not necessary to have academics come to Germany to work on an assembly line. They were trained on the job.

Given temporary visas, the Germans expected the workers to come, make money and then head home. Instead the men stayed and then brought their families — along with their traditions, religion and culture. The immigrants settled together and neighborhoods began to reflect their new inhabitants. Signs were hung in Turkish, supermarkets sold Turkish products and stands selling kebabs sandwiches popped up everywhere.

These immigrants arrived during the collapse of sexual morality in the West. It was a shock for these people, so of course, they put up borders. They felt, they don't want us here, and we don't want to be like them; they are immoral. Then German industry changed requiring more qualified workers; the jobs filled by many of these laborers disappeared, leading to widespread unemployment.

Many Muslim women in Germany have arranged marriages. Parents take their daughters back to Turkey to visit a gynecologist to establish that they are still virgins. When the parents' worst nightmare is confirmed, the daughters are damaged goods, their prospects ruined and the family shamed.

The US Liberal Pussy Cat

US Liberals like to play the blame game but have undermined any meaningful US foreign policy.

The CIA strongly suspected North Korea had developed nuclear weapons as far back as the early 1990s. It both signed and defied the Nuclear Non-Proliferation Treaty (NPT), which prohibits acquiring bombs. It formally withdrew and has now tested a nuclear device.

Direct talks between Washington and Pyongyang will not achieve a settlement. North Korea violated the last such settlement, the so-called

"Yongbyong Agreed Framework" of 1994. North Korea cannot be trusted to honor their commitments or cajoled into abandoning their weapons.

For more than two decades, the USA and its allies have blinked at North Korea's nuclear-weapons activities, even when they clearly violated international treaties that Pyongyang had signed. The United Nations and the USA bent the nuclear rules to accommodate North Korea's misbehavior and groveled repeatedly before Pyongyang and Beijing to keep this duplicitous diplomacy afloat.

The USA first blinked almost as soon as it discovered Pyongyang's construction of a military production reactor at Yongbyong in 1984. The reactor had no hook-up with any portion of North Korea's electrical grid, yet we decided to act as if it did. In 1985, with Soviet help, we got Pyongyang to sign the NPT. The treaty requires that new members complete an agreement with the International Atomic Energy Agency (IAEA) within 18 months. When Pyongyang failed to do so, we again blinked repeatedly for six years. To get Pyongyang to sign, we finally acceded in 1991 to North Korean demands that the U.S. first remove its tactical nuclear weapons from South Korea and allow North Korea to inspect South Korean military bases.

Washington did persuade Pyongyang and Seoul to agree not to reprocess or enrich uranium or to acquire nuclear weapons. Pyongyang violated this agreement immediately. The IAEA confirmed this point after their first inspections revealed Pyongyang had reprocessed some of its spent fuel. After Pyongyang refused IAEA requests for further inspections, the IAEA referred the matter to the United Nations Security Council, which was ready to impose sanctions against North Korea.

The Clinton Administration blocked UN sanctions action with a generous offer of energy assistance, including a promise of two large light water reactors along with a suspension of routine IAEA inspections. In exchange, Pyongyang was asked to promise eventually to come back into compliance with its NPT and IAEA obligations. For nearly a decade Pyongyang did no such thing. When the Bush administration finally discovered Pyongyang was cheating on its pledge not to make nuclear weapons-usable fuel, the White House suspended further energy assistance and the IAEA again referred North Korea's case to the Security Council.

The USA, under Liberal pressure to use multination diplomacy, called for multilateral talks with North Korea, Japan, South Korea, Russia and China to get Pyongyang to voluntarily disarm. The USA had to plead with North Korea and China to cooperate (Pyongyang to come and Beijing to pressure Pyongyang to behave). It did not work and since we are such a pussy cat what we do next will not work either.

Democrats have stated that Kim Jong-Il's latest demonstration of aggressive intent "illustrates just how much the Bush Administration's incompetence has endangered our nation. The President provoked North Korea into building a bomb by naming it to the axis of evil".

"Bush aided and abetted the outsourcing of American jobs," said Democratic Party chairman Howard Dean, "and now he's outsourced our diplomacy as well."

Jimmy Carter in an article in the New York Times blamed the Bush Administration but failed to mention that North Korea played both of the Carter and Clinton Administrations for fools in violating all agreements. How dishonest is Jimmy and how dishonest is the New York Times as always?

The Democrats will not even allow the confirmation of Ambassador Bolton to the UN even though he is an expert on non-proliferation and is not a pussy cat but is a skilled negotiator. He is undermined by having to operate as a probationer by US Liberals.

Imagine the mess that we will be in when these Liberal apologists are in control.

Why US Liberals are so dangerous

We needn't give credence to the assertion of President Bush that terrorist would turn up in our cities if we pulled up stakes from Baghdad to recognize that a terrible price would be paid were we to opt for a hasty and unseemly withdrawal from Iraq. The Middle East has a keen eye for the weakness of strangers. The heated debate about the origins of our drive into Iraq would surely pale by comparison to the debate that would erupt were we to give in to despair and cast the Iraqis adrift. US Liberals do not even begin to understand how naïve they are.

Now US Liberals are intent on the blame game over North Korea. Guess whose fault it is in their editorials? The real culprits of course are US Liberals, who have so emasculated the US abroad by perpetual undermining US foreign policy that no rogue country takes the US seriously as the world's policeman. As a consequence of Foley, Liberals will soon have even more power to undermine US credibility abroad. The American electorate is also seemingly a lost cause and will reap the whirlwind of its distorted priorities.

Countries like North Korea and Iran seek nuclear weapons because they imagine that those weapons will enhance their security and power. The way to contain them is to convince them otherwise. Prevention by nonproliferation is always to be preferred. But when negotiation fails, as it has failed in North Korea and is failing in Iran, rogue regimes must be made to suffer for their dangerous nuclear ambitions. The US Liberal pussy cat is unable and unwilling to do that.

Paper Tiger

The USA has once again voted against continuing a conflict it previously endorsed, demonstrating yet again that it does not have the stomach for armed conflict if the going gets tough, as it inevitably does. Now all is blamed on President Bush, even though the decision to depose Saddam Hussein had unanimity in the USA. One conclusion clearly is that the USA should never again lead the West into conflict, which probably means that there is no longer a super power to police the world. As a consequence, this repudiation of George Bush is a victory for terrorists and rogue regimes, throughout the world.

It is a pyrrhic victory for all the Liberals around the world who despise US might.

In a joint statement, more than 200 members of the European Parliament hailed the American 2006 election results as "the beginning of the end of a six-year nightmare for the world" and gloated that they left the Bush administration "seriously weakened."

The UK's Guardian newspaper wrote: "The cheering can be heard not just in America itself but around the planet."

European Liberals will quickly find that much-needed American influence to resolve European and global problems has been severely compromised. The big losers will be Europe, which is even less likely now to reverse its terminal decline. US Liberals have shown that the USA is a paper tiger because it cannot sustain world leadership in the face of even modest losses, reversals and unpopularity.

The USA can no longer be regarded as the world leader. It is the end of the beginning for the USA. The new world order, starting with China, will begin to assert itself.

Liberal Distortion

What a sad day for the United States, and for the rest of the world witnessing this event, that a bill has been signed into law that allows torture. Yes, the United States has been a shining light of freedom and democracy; now it is quickly becoming a rogue state, characterized by a lust for war, hoping to achieve the quelling of dissent by indoctrination inside the United States and by violence outside of it.

Kees Schepers, Antwerp, Belgium

We could leave Iraq honorably by immediately withdrawing all our armed forces and turning over to the United Nations all the money we've allotted to the war, to be administered by the United Nations as the Iraqis desire. The Iraqis would get back their oil and could rebuild the infrastructure — electricity, sewage, schools, hospitals, water treatment — that the Bush administration has destroyed in their tragic country. Once Iraq and the world have seen that we are genuinely trying to make amends for the evil we have strewn there, we might slowly regain the world's good opinion, which this administration forfeited.

Mary Steele, Cambridge, MA.

To admit that the war is going badly, even to admit to a couple of mistakes, cannot have been easy for such an inflexible individual as Bush, who is unreceptive to what some in his administration sometimes derisively call reality. The mistakes that Bush admitted to -- not anticipating that the Iraqi Army would melt away and that civil servants wouldn't show up for work when American troops entered Baghdad -- are but a tiny fraction compared with the many errors now being documented in dozens of new books. The books agree that the Bush administration entered Iraq like a dim-witted child stumbling into a Middle Eastern bazaar and smashing things. America's performance has been so pathetic that one hardly knows whether to laugh or to cry.

Greenway, Boston Globe

Capital Punishment

Governor Jon Corzine has signed legislation repealing capital punishment in New Jersey.

In what The New York Times called "an extended and often passionate speech," Corzine praised the members of the Death Penalty Study Commission who had recommended repeal. He saluted the "courageous leadership" of the state legislators who had voted for it, mentioning eight of them by name. He thanked New Jerseyans for Alternatives to the Death Penalty, an activist group, for having "put pressure on those of us in public service to stand up and do the right thing." He proclaimed himself "eternally grateful" to other anti-death-penalty organizations, especially the New Jersey Catholic Conference and the ACLU. He acknowledged "the millions of people across our nation and around the globe who reject the death penalty."

He did not mention -

Kristin Huggins. She was the 22-year-old graphic artist kidnapped in 1992 by Ambrose Harris, who stuffed her into the trunk of her car, then let her out in order to rape her and shoot her twice - once in the back of her head, once point-blank in the face.

Irene Schnaps, a 37-year-old widow butchered by Nathaniel Harvey in 1985. After breaking into her apartment and robbing her, he killed her with 15 blows to the head, using a "hammer-like" weapon with such violence that he fractured her skull, broke her jaw, and knocked out her teeth.

Megan Kanka, just 7 years old when she was murdered by a neighbor, Jesse Timmendequas. A convicted sex offender, Timmendequas lured Megan into his house by offering to show her a puppy. Then he raped her, smashed her into a dresser, wrapped plastic bags around her head and strangled her with a belt.

The governor did not mention any of the victims murdered by the men on New Jersey's death row. Liberal death-penalty opponents like Corzine have consciences which are outraged by the death penalty, but consciences which can ignore the additional lives lost when capital punishment is eliminated.

Since New Jersey hasn't executed anyone since 1963, the new law is largely symbolic. But there is nothing symbolic about all the blood shed since the death penalty was abandoned 44 years ago. In 1963, there were 181 homicides in the Garden State. By 1970 there were more than 400, and by 1980, more than 500. In 2002, state officials calculated that on average, a murder was committed in New Jersey every 25 hours and 41 minutes.

While the murder rate since 2000 has declined modestly across the country, it has "jumped 44 percent in Jersey, up from 3.4 murders per 100,000 people to 4.9," writes Steven Malanga of the Manhattan Institute. "Jersey's increase in murders has been the sixth-highest in the country."

53 percent of the state's residents opposed the death-penalty repeal, according to a new Quinnipiac poll, while 78 percent favored retaining it for "the most violent cases." They grasp the truth that eludes Liberal politicians. The death penalty for those who are merciless killers saves innocent lives.

Liberals who oppose capital punishment assert that an execution has no deterrent effect on future crimes. To the contrary, the death penalty has an enormous deterrent effect on the number of murders. More precisely, recent research shows that each US execution correlates with 74 fewer murders the following year.

The study examined the relationship between the number of executions and the number of murders in the USA for the 26-year period from 1979 to 2004, using data from publicly available FBI sources. When executions increase, murders decrease, and when executions decrease, murders increase. In the early 1980s, the return of the death penalty was associated with a drop in the number of murders. In the mid-to-late 1980s, when the number of executions stabilized at about 20 per year, the number of murders increased. Throughout the 1990s, our society increased the number of executions, and the number of murders plummeted. Since 2001, there has been a decline in executions and an increase in murders.

University of Houston professors Dale Cloninger and Roberto Marchesini studied the effect of the death-penalty moratorium declared by Illinois Governor George Ryan in 2000, and Ryan's subsequent commutation of every death-row inmate's sentence. An estimated 150 additional murders in Illinois were committed over the subsequent 48 months.

The conclusion that each execution carried out is associated with the saving of dozens of innocent lives should create a moral dilemma for Liberals who campaign against the death penalty. Instead of feeling good for having "saved a life" when executions are overturned, they should be concerned much more about the lives of dozens of future murder victims.

CHAPTER 8
MEDIA

Contributions of the Boston Globe to the War on Terror

The Boston Globe continually attacks the Bush Administration with its Liberal Opinions. It is less a newspaper than a left wing propaganda sheet. It has the same ownership as the New York Times and the same Liberal stance. Unlike the New York Times it is not well written and is not used as the vehicle to leak damaging, secret and classified information. Instead it likes to invent Republican policy and positions and then attack them. It is painful to read. The following are two recent extracts.

"Unlike many Bush critics on the left, I don't believe that this administration is made up of villains who want to rape the Constitution, slaughter and torture brown-skinned people in the Middle East, and reduce the American people to a mass of compliant sheep. It seems likely to me that Bush and many of those around him are motivated by good intentions, but these good intentions have been coupled with an arrogance of power that may yet take us down the proverbial road to hell."

Cathy Young

"To-day, the ideological heirs to the lunatic fringe are running the American government. Every arrogant miscalculation only leads them to more disastrous blunders. In Iraq, where Saddam turned out to be telling the truth (about nuclear weapons) and Bush turned out to be lying, diplomacy was forsaken for war. Had Bush used diplomacy to isolate Saddam and to improve relations with Iran and Syria, had he worked as Bill Clinton did for a reduction of violence and a true peace process between Israelis and Palestinians, radical Islam would have far less appeal, the United States would have more influence in the world, and Israel would be more secure. But you can't undo history, and the mess Bush made will haunt his successors for decades. Will voters finally recognize that this crowd is delusionally incompetent? Or will cynical fear-mongering lead anxious citizens yet again to rally round their president?"

Robert Kuttner

By justifying our enemies, by casting them as victims and by labeling the Bush Administration as villains, lunatics, liars, power hungry war mongers and delusional incompetents, US Liberals empower our enemies and endanger the USA

Action and Reaction are Equal and Opposite

As leaks through the New York Times go, those based on classified information cause the biggest ruckus. It's impossible to know how true their latest intelligence leak is, since the 2006 National Intelligence Estimate hasn't been leaked. The reports are based on what the New York Times claims the NIE says from unidentified sources, but we don't know who those sources are and what motivations they might have. Since their spin coincides rather conveniently with the argument made by Liberal critics of the war, and since this leak has also conveniently been reported by the New York Times in high campaign season, all but Liberals will be skeptical.

According to the New York Times the Iraq war has made overall terrorism worse, supposedly because the war has provoked radical Islamists to hate America even more than they already did before they hijacked airplanes and flew them into buildings. When will Liberals get it into their heads that radical Islamists in large numbers hate us for who we are in our decadent Liberal world, based on their religious teachings?

The President has now been forced to declassify the relevant parts of the NIE to counter false accusations. Indeed the one thing the reports do not say is that war in Iraq has made terrorism worse. This declassification is not enough for the Liberals who now want the President to declassify the entire NIE, including sensitive raw intelligence. Some passages will compromise sources and methods and would give terrorists a valuable window into the thinking that goes on at places like the CIA.

As for the substance of the 2006 NIE's alleged claims, it is inevitable and obvious that terrorists have rallied against the American presence in Iraq. Indeed al-Qaeda is complaining that over 4000 of foreign born terrorists have been killed in Iraq. In other words, they are being sucked into Iraq where our troops are dealing with them on the battle field of our choice, which is far preferable than them attacking us on US soil. Whether the war in Iraq has produced more external terrorist activity than would otherwise exist, however, is a matter of opinion and strategic judgment.

One of Osama bin Laden's justifications for declaring war against the U.S. was American enforcement of sanctions and a no-fly zone against Iraq before the 2003 invasion. Originally it was having our troops in Saudi Arabia when we were fighting Saddam Hussein after he had invaded Kuwait. More broadly, the liberation of Iraq and Afghanistan has deprived the terrorist of two safe havens and sources of funds. So while there are still many al Qaeda-type terror cells out there, there's no reason to believe they are any more dangerous now than before April 2003. Abu Musab al-Zarqawi, one of the terrorists harbored in Iraq before the war, certainly isn't any more dangerous; he's dead.

Iraq is the central front in the war on terror, and withdrawing our troops would confirm to the world and to the terrorists, once again, that the US has no staying power and that we are wimps when it comes to hanging tough under difficult circumstances. Our withdrawal would create a vacuum that the Islamists will fill giving them a new base of operations to export terrorism. That's the choice voters ought to be thinking about as they go to the polls in November.

We need to understand scientific principles and then we would know that action and reaction are equal and opposite. This particular leak by the New York Times actually tells us nothing other than that they are increasingly subversive.

We have now reached the point where the Liberal Media is the fourth branch of Government. Our political system is already dysfunctional and is being undermined by Liberals who are peeved that they are out of power. Subversion by the Liberal media is a major problem.

Intelligence is supposed to provide information on important military and political trends, and act as a check on policy makers' assumptions and beliefs. Forcing intelligence into the public arena as Liberals and their media are doing will make it almost impossible to perform these roles, which is another victory Liberals are handing to the terrorists.

The Last Vestiges of Free Speech and a Truthful Media in Britain

The trouble with looking for a critic in the British media is that normal intellectual standards are collapsing. Even the once-respected BBC has admitted to fixing competitions and deceiving its viewers as a matter of routine. There is a corresponding collapse in other institutions. A recent headline that an Oxford Union debate was disrupted by protestors is only to be expected in Liberal (once Great) Britain.

Protesters broke through a security cordon and forced their way into the Oxford Union where Nick Griffin, leader of the far-Right BNP party, and David Irving, the controversial historian, were due to debate the limits of free speech.

After pushing and shoving their way through the doors into the hall, around 20 demonstrators staged a sit down protest and began chanting at the debating table.

The debate eventually began one-and-a-half hours late, with Liberal Democrat MP Evan Harris and journalist Anne Atkins speaking against Mr. Irving in one room whilst two Oxford University post-graduate students took on Mr. Griffin in another.

Fearing bloody clashes between the protesters and far-right groups Thames Valley Police had drafted in large numbers of officers to control the demonstration.

Invitations to Mr. Irving and Mr. Griffin prompted outrage. Tory MP Julian Lewis, shadow defense minister resigned his lifetime membership of the society saying he was ashamed of the students' decision.

Mr. Irving has been jailed in Austria for denying the holocaust but pleading guilty, he told the court: "I made a mistake when I said there were no gas chambers at Auschwitz."

In his speech the historian insisted his account of events is based on the evidence available. "I still refuse to be bowed I am not going to write what they want me to write I'm going to write what I find in the archives," he said.

Mr. Griffin has been convicted for incitement to racial hatred but has repeatedly claimed his party is not racist. He compared protestors objecting to his appearance in Oxford with Adolf Hitler's supporters: "This is a mob which would kill. I have seen them beat old men and women and try to kill them. Had they grown up in Nazi Germany they would have made splendid Nazis."

The president of the Union, Luke Tryl, claimed that the event had achieved the result he hoped for. "I think David Irving came out of that looking pathetic," he said. "I said in my introduction that I found his view repugnant and abhorrent because I wanted that on record."

Nick Griffin was born in Barnet and grew up in Halesworth in rural Suffolk, England. Initially educated at two Suffolk public schools, St Felix School (in Southwold) and Woodbridge School, Griffin studied history and then law at Downing College, Cambridge. Griffin boxed while at Cambridge and became a boxing blue. He graduated with a third class degree in History with Law (Tripos I History 2 years/ Tripos II Law 1 year). Since leaving university, Griffin has worked in agricultural engineering, property renovation and forestry. In recent years he has been a full-time political writer and organizer of the British National Party, of which he is chairman. Griffin's mother, Jean (nee Thomas), was the BNP candidate against Iain Duncan Smith at the 2001 Election, and his father, Edgar, was a member of the Conservative Party and a former councilor. In August 2001, Edgar Griffin was expelled from the Conservative Party. At the time, he had been vice-president of Iain Duncan Smith's party leadership election campaign in Wales.

In 1998, Griffin, along with Paul Ballard, was convicted of violating section 19 of the Public Order Act 1986, relating to incitement to racial hatred, for his editorship of issue 12 of The Rune, published in 1996.The complaint regarding the magazine was made by Alex Carlile QC, who was the Liberal Democrat MP for Montgomeryshire at the time. He had asked the police to obtain him a copy of the magazine, which they did.

After reading it, the MP called the police again and complained about its content, whereupon the police raided Griffin's home and charged him. He was convicted and received a nine-month prison sentence, suspended for two years, and was fined £2,300. This conviction has been said to be contradictory to Griffin's outspoken demands for "law & order", although Griffin claims that the law under which he was convicted "is an unjust law and he therefore has no obligation to follow it".

On 14 December 2004, Nick Griffin was arrested on suspicion of incitement to racial hatred, relating to a BBC documentary broadcast in July 2004, in which he was recorded at Morley Town Hall (in a constituency which later went on to elect a BNP councilor in 2006) as saying that Islam was a "...wicked and vicious faith". He was the 12th person to be arrested following the documentary and the second most prominent after BNP founder John Tyndall, who had been arrested two days earlier. Griffin was released on police bail the same day but, the following April, was charged with four offences of using words or behavior intended or likely to stir up racial hatred.

On 6 February 2006, a jury at Leeds Crown Court returned not guilty verdicts on two of the charges and was unable to reach a verdict on the other two. The Crown Prosecution Service announced that it would seek a re-trial.

In early November 2006, the retrial of Griffin and co-defendant Mark Collett took place and once again both men were found not guilty on all counts, which means that of all the people arrested in connection with the BBC documentary none had been convicted of any offence relating to it. Somewhat controversially, Government ministers have since called for a review of existing laws.

After the trial, Griffin celebrated outside the court with over two hundred supporters and champagne in red, white and blue bottles donated by Jean-Marie Le Pen. "What has just happened shows Tony Blair and the government toadies at the BBC that they can take our taxes but they cannot take our hearts, they cannot take our tongues and they cannot take our freedom," he told his supporters.

Free Speech and Hate Speech

Hate speech is a term for speech intended to degrade, intimidate, or incite violence or prejudicial action against a person or group of people based on their race, gender, age, ethnicity, nationality, religion, sexual orientation, gender identity, disability, language ability, moral or political views, socioeconomic class, occupation or appearance (such as height, weight, and hair color), mental capacity and any other distinction-liability. The term covers written as well as oral communication and some forms of behaviors in a public setting. It is also sometimes called anti-locution and is the first point on Allport's scale which measures prejudice in a society.

In the United States, government is broadly forbidden by the First Amendment of the Constitution from restricting speech. Jurists generally understand this to mean that the government cannot regulate the content of speech, but that it can address the harmful effects of speech through laws such as those against defamation or incitement to riot.

Since such laws often apply only to the victimization of specific individuals, some argue that hate speech must be regulated to protect members of groups. Others argue that hate speech limits the free development of political discourse and ought to be regulated, but by voluntary actions and not by the state. Still others claim that it is not possible to legislate a boundary between legitimate controversial speech and hate speech.

Where such laws exist they are limited by the constitutional rights to freedom of expression. For example, the German constitution is subtly more restrictive, guaranteeing 'freedom of voicing one's opinion' and elsewhere restricts its misuse against the public peace. The German Criminal Code specifically forbids inciting hatred against ethnic groups, and revisionism, as in France under the Gayssot Act, is prohibited under those grounds.

The Liberal Media around the World

Since CNN and BBC are the voices of the USA and UK around the world it is no wonder that we are so despised; they constantly show the

USA and UK in a poor light compared with their enemies which are always handled deferentially. The leader of Hamas is interviewed with great respect as he lambastes Israel and the USA. In the eyes of viewers worldwide who do not have our freedoms, it is confirmation of how bad the Bush Administration is since even our own press condemns what it does and is sympathetic to Hamas and other organizations considered terrorists by the USA and UK.

The message is that Hamas is OK and we have unreasonable expectations. The Palestinians in turn think that they are being treated unfairly for exercising their democratic rights by voting Hamas into power. They avoid the inconvenient realization that there are consequences to supporting terrorism and working to overthrow the Israeli hand that feeds them. CNN, BBC and the New York Times routinely vindicate them and Al-Jazeera, advised by BBC executives, is the voice of our enemies including Hamas and al-Qaeda.

Hollywood has taken to glorifying suicide bombing and terrorism under the guise of seeking understanding. They depict suicide bombers not as evil, but likeable humans. In their casting, the bomber characters are heroes deserving of our sympathy. Hollywood explains that they are seeking to portray the underlying human personality. What they are doing is depicting Western norms of personality. They have no way of looking into or understanding the depraved, tortured and twisted minds of Islamic suicide bombers and how they are being duped and brainwashed by fanatics such as Hamas. Hollywood has become another propaganda vehicle, just like the Liberal media for our enemies to use.

CNN's former news executive, Jordan Eason, acknowledged after the fall of Saddam Hussein that his network had long sanitized its news from Iraq, since reporting the unvarnished truth "would have jeopardized the lives of our Baghdad staff."

The Islam fascists are emboldened by appeasement and submissiveness.

The BBC, CNN, New York Times, Boston Globe and all their fellow travelers betray ideals that generations of Americans and Britons have died to defend.

What we need is not appeasement and apologies and a dread of giving offense by our Liberal media. We must not be intimidated by bullies and must face down fanatics. In the global struggle against Islamist extremism, we need a media voice of courage that leads the way. Our Achilles heel is the broad distribution worldwide of the BBC and CNN with no other channels for us to get out the truth.

The Liberal media likes to fuel the flames against the West. Equally they are selective in the news that they report. They do not report stories critical of Muslims or Islam. One story that was not told is that of Jihad Momani, editor of the Jordanian newspaper Shihan. He published three of the Danish Cartoons of Islam with an appeal. "Muslims of the world be reasonable," he wrote, "What brings more prejudice against Islam, these caricatures or pictures of a hostage-taker slashing the throats of his victims in front of the cameras or a suicide bomber who blows himself up during a wedding ceremony in Amman?" Momani was sacked. He apologized. He was arrested nevertheless and has disappeared. This unreported story by the Liberal media also tells us something else. There are moderate Muslims but they are silenced. In Nazi Germany, there were moderate Germans who were silenced also.

It is undeniable that Muslims treat women in a bizarre manner. At breakfast in a hotel in Asia, I observed a diminutive Muslim woman with only her eyes showing, feeding herself by taking food inside her clothing at navel level and then trying to get it to her mouth. After the meal, she left dutifully, two steps behind her burly husband. The breakfast was a buffet, but the woman's food, the little she ate, was brought to her by her husband, who stuffed himself mightily. In the West, this treatment would be considered to be abusive.

Former Australian Prime Minister John Howard expressed concern about extremist Muslim immigrants in Australia bent on Jihad. Muslims constitute 1.5% of 20 million Australians. Howard's remarks followed violence and inappropriate behavior towards women on a Sydney beach by Lebanese-Australians. Howard added that some Muslim attitudes towards women are not appropriate in Australia. His remarks led to criticism from Muslims but he is one world leader who is unwilling to back down, whatever the media says.

CHAPTER 9
LIES, PROPAGANDA, INTELLIGENCE FAILURES

Did The President Lie to Go to War?

It is gravely insulting to suggest that a US President would justify a war based on information he knows to be false and which would be shown to be false within months after the war concluded. US Liberals though continuously parrot that he did lie. This falsehood is now accepted fact.

Kennedy, Carter and Gore are key perpetrators. Their recent statements are that:

"Bush misled the nation and led us into a quagmire in Iraq" Ted Kennedy.

"President Bush has not been honest with the American people on Iraq." Jimmy Carter.

"An abuse of the truth characterized the administration's march to war." Al Gore.

In the run up to Operation Iraqi Freedom everyone was operating from the same set of assumptions regarding Iraq's weapons of mass destruction (WMD) capabilities. Important assumptions turned out wrong; but mistakenly relying on faulty intelligence is not the same as lying about it.

The National Intelligence Estimate (NIE), the intelligence community's authoritative judgment stated that:

"Iraq has continued its WMD programs in defiance of U.N. resolutions and restrictions. Baghdad has chemical and biological weapons as well as missiles with ranges in excess of U.N. restrictions; if left unchecked, it probably will have a nuclear weapon during this decade."

Based on this information -

John Kerry said, "I believe that a deadly arsenal of weapons of mass destruction in Saddam Hussein's hands is a threat, and a grave threat, to our security."

Sen. Kennedy said, "We have known for many years that Saddam Hussein is seeking and developing weapons of mass destruction."

Hillary Clinton said "Intelligence reports show that Saddam Hussein has worked to rebuild his chemical and biological weapons stock, his missile delivery capability and his nuclear program."

The German ambassador said, "I think all of our governments believe that Iraq has produced weapons of mass destruction and that we have to assume that they continue to have weapons of mass destruction."

Iraqis can participate in three historic elections, pass the most liberal constitution in the Arab world, and form a unity government despite terrorist attacks and provocations. Yet for the President's detractors, these are minor matters.

Did George Bush Pressure Intelligence Agencies to Bias their Judgments?

The Liberals repeatedly say that the President pressured Intelligence Agencies to provide biased information to allow him to go to war with Iraq. Recently Al Gore and Ted Kennedy have made these allegations.

"CIA analysts who strongly disagreed with the White House found themselves under pressure at work and became fearful of losing promotions and salary increases." Al Gore.

"The Administration put pressure on intelligence officers to produce the desired intelligence and analysis." Senator Kennedy.

The facts are quite different. The Senate Select Committee on Intelligence's Bipartisan Report stated that -

"The committee did not find any evidence that intelligence analysts changed their judgments as a result of political pressure, altered or produced intelligence products to conform with administration policy, or that anyone even attempted to coerce, influence or pressure analysts to do so."

Air Force Gen. Michael Hayden complained that intelligence-gathering has become a football in American political discourse. "For the past few years, the intelligence community and the CIA have taken an inordinate number of hits, some of them fair, many of them not," Hayden said at his Senate confirmation hearing.

Democratic Sen. Carl Levin of Michigan complained about the CIA's recent past.

In an opening statement, Levin suggested that in the run-up to Iraq, intelligence had been manipulated to support the administration's desire to overthrow Saddam Hussein.

Committee Chairman Sen. Pat Roberts of Kansas complained about the CIA's performance on Iraq. While "nobody bats 1,000 in the intelligence world," Roberts cited "a terribly flawed trade craft" in the CIA's intelligence suggesting the presence of weapons of mass destruction there.

Hayden acknowledged a series of intelligence failures in the run-up to the U.S. decision to invade Iraq and promised to take steps to guard against a repeat of such errors. "We just took too much for granted. We didn't challenge our basic assumptions."

The CIA has also been compromised by partisan insiders leaking classified information. Their allegiances should be to the U.S. government in the name of national security. By leaking classified information as they have, they have undermined President Bush and his efforts to effectively fight the War on Terror.

With an enemy as vast as the one we are facing now, it is to be hoped that we have seen the last of such egregious occurrences. The American people can ill afford any more CIA employees placing partisan personal interests before their ever important duties in gathering intelligence and keeping us safe from future terrorist attacks.

Is Promoting Democracy in the Middle East a Postwar Rationalization?

Liberals are now trying to pretend that promoting democracy in the Middle East is an afterthought.

"The President now says that the war is really about the spread of democracy in the Middle East. This effort at after-the-fact justification was only made necessary because the primary rationale was so sadly lacking in fact." Nancy Pelosi.

The truth is that President Bush argued repeatedly for democracy taking root in Iraq before the war began.

"A liberated Iraq can show the power of freedom to transform that vital region, by bringing hope and progress into the lives of millions. America's interests in security, and America's belief in liberty, both lead in the same direction: to a free and peaceful Iraq. The world has a clear interest in the spread of democratic values, because stable and free nations do not breed the ideologies of murder. They encourage the peaceful pursuit of a better life. And there are hopeful signs of a desire for freedom in the Middle East. A new regime in Iraq would serve as a dramatic and inspiring example of freedom for other nations in the region."

For many antiwar critics, the president is faulted for the war, and he, not the former dictator of Iraq, inspires rage. The liberator rather than the oppressor provokes hatred. It is as if we have stepped through the political looking glass, into a world turned upside down and inside out.

Spreading falsehoods is the only contribution of US Liberals. A test of our character is if we are ready for political leaders who don't pander, who are willing to talk about complicated issues and call for responsible policies.

Rep. John Murtha

The Profiles in Courage Award has been awarded to Rep. John Murtha, a Pennsylvania Democrat and former marine who has become a fierce critic of the Iraq war, He has unleashed a firestorm by saying to a broad audience that he has no doubts that marines killed innocent civilians in Haditha and tried to cover up the deaths. Marine Corps officials, he said in one television interview, have told him that troops shot one woman "in cold blood" while bending over her child begging for mercy. Murtha got his information by maintaining close ties with senior Marine officers, who are fellow travelers opposed to the police action in Iraq.

"Our troops overreacted because of the pressure on them, and they killed innocent civilians in cold blood." said Rep. John Murtha, D-Pa., publicizing his comments widely, even though the case is still under investigation and no charges have been filed. Murtha's real target is George Bush and he excuses the actions of the marines by saying that they are unable to cope with the stress. Murtha is a prominent critic of Bush administration policies in Iraq. He repeated his view that the war in Iraq cannot be won militarily and needs political solutions.

When he was presented with the Award, John Murtha was lauded as a member of Congress and Vietnam veteran, for "making a difficult decision of conscience last year when he reversed his support for the Iraq war and sparked a national debate by calling for the immediate withdrawal of US troops from the conflict."

The currently emerging Liberal spin on the story about what happened in Haditha, where at least two dozen Iraqi men, women and children were apparently shot by a small group of American marines, is that this deplorable situation is only the latest indication of what terrible things can happen when soldiers are required to occupy hostile civilian territory in the midst of an armed insurrection and looming civil war. A military investigation is currently deciding whether any of the marines should be charged with murder, and whether a cover-up took place. All these questions have awful resonance for those who remember Vietnam, and what that prolonged and ultimately pointless war did to both the Vietnamese and the American social fabric.

These words are synonymous with military disgrace. The My Lai massacre was the beginning of the end for the USA in Vietnam. Haditha, as publicized by Murtha, could be the bell tolling for the USA in Iraq. Already Prime Minister Nuri Kamal al-Maliki has lashed out at the American military, denouncing what he characterized as habitual attacks by troops against Iraqi civilians. Nuri Maliki said violence against civilians had become a daily phenomenon by many of our troops who do not respect the Iraqi people.

Murtha, by publicizing and politicizing Haditha, is causing enormous damage to the USA. It gives him momentary glory with his fellow Liberals, but his actions are not Profiles in Courage.

Murtha has opened the Floodgates

"This is a phenomenon that has become common among many of the multinational forces. No respect for citizens, smashing civilian cars and killing on a suspicion or a hunch. It's unacceptable." Said Iraqi Prime Minister Nouri al-Maliki, on human rights violations by coalition forces in Iraq

New video footage from the northern town of Ishaqi shows the bodies of several Iraqi civilians, including children, who were killed during a US raid on a house in March. Pentagon officials said an inquiry into the case had found that US forces used appropriate force in the attack on what they called a terrorist hideout.

Iraqi officials condemned the event in March, but it had faded from view until yesterday, when video images of the aftermath of the US operation in Ishaqi set off a new round of criticism of American treatment of civilians on the battlefield.

The Ishaqi case was the third accusation in a week involving alleged misconduct by US forces in Iraq, fueling angry reactions by Iraqi officials. On Thursday, US military officials said they expect eight

Marines and one Navy medic to face murder charges for executing an Iraqi in the town of Hamandiya, west of Baghdad in April.

US soldiers fired into a car at a checkpoint, killing a pregnant Iraqi woman and her mother. They wounded another woman at another checkpoint. In both cases, the military said the occupants of the cars failed to heed warnings that the road was closed. In the double fatality, the surviving driver and the pregnant woman's brother told the Los Angeles Times, "I took this road because it's a shortcut and my sister was in labor. I was surprised by the exploding glass and blood coming from behind. When I turned back, my sister was shot in the head."

The BBC has aired video footage of the bodies of 11 civilians, including four women, one as old as 75, and five children, one as young as 6 months. They were killed in March. The US military said that as troops approached a suspected Al Qaeda safe house, they were fired on and responded with a massive ground and air assault. The report said they apprehended the target of the operation that killed one man, two women, and a child. It said the heavy fire collapsed the roof.

But locals, including Iraqi police, told a very different story. People said that an Al Qaeda member was visiting relatives. But they said the house was still standing when US soldiers entered to inspect it. They said soldiers rounded up the 11 people, members of a schoolteacher's family, and coldly executed them. The BBC has reiterated what locals said at the time, that the dead had bullet wounds, and showed no signs of being crushed by a collapsed roof.

A huge part of the problem is that the USA never did learn its lessons from My Lai where 500 Vietnamese were massacred. In the end, there was virtually no accountability and no punishment for the killings. The only soldier convicted, Lieutenant William Calley, had his sentence reduced to relative insignificance by President Nixon, and was released after three years of house arrest. He went on to sell jewelry in Georgia.

US mommies worry excessively, but only about their offspring. No one really cares about the innocent from other cultures. Until we do that we should confine our Ugliness to the USA. So said one –

"My son, a 19-year-old American marine, is scheduled to be sent on the "deadly fool's errand" to Iraq in September. I live with constant fear that he, too, will be pointlessly injured, maimed or killed in this "obvious quagmire." Unspeakable horrors, as in the town of Haditha, are creating victims of both innocent Iraqis and young Americans being exploited for their patriotic ideals by leaders who support the war but don't, in fact, support the troops.I have opposed the war since its beginning. Now, three years on, with my own son's participation in it looming, I'm living the ultimate nightmare where I'm screaming and no one — but no one — is listening."

Massachusetts and Vermont

Brookline and Cambridge, MA

John F. Kennedy was born in Brookline, MA, a town which is providing aid and comfort to Terrorists. Brookline has followed the lead of Cambridge and a handful of communities in Vermont by Town Meeting members voting 104 to 52, to call on the state's congressional representatives to impeach President Bush. The resolution declared that Bush has repeatedly violated his oath of office by purposely misleading the country as he launched the war in Iraq.

Brattleboro, VT

Brattleboro, during its town meeting, passed an ordinance that would allow the town's police to arrest President Bush or Vice President Cheney for war crimes if they were ever to come to Vermont. It is not surprising that Vermont is the only state that George Bush has not visited in the past eight years.

Curveball

Curveball's fraudulent claims were largely responsible for the pre-Iraq War view that Saddam Hussein possessed biological weapons. Now the German magazine Der Spiegel has told us about the spy who lied.

Curveball is Rafid Ahmed Alwan, an opportunistic Iraqi asylum-seeker who came to Germany in 1999. His claims to having inside knowledge of Saddam's illicit weapons program quickly made him a prized asset of Germany's intelligence service, the BND. So convinced were the Germans of the reliability of his information that in the fall of 2001 they purchased 35 million doses of smallpox vaccine for fear of what Saddam might do.

More remarkable is that even after September 11 – when then-Chancellor Gerhard Schröder promised "infinite solidarity" with the U.S. – the German government refused to allow the CIA to interview Curveball in person. Often, the Germans resorted to dishonest pretexts for their lack of cooperation, such as that Curveball didn't speak English, when in fact he spoke it fluently (and as if nobody in the CIA spoke German or Arabic). "It was a blockade that made it impossible for any other service to validate his information," David Kay, who ran the Iraq Survey Group that looked for WMD after the war, told Der Spiegel.

BND nonetheless sent some 100 reports about Curveball's information to the CIA. And while doubts about Curveball's credibility began to emerge on both sides of the Atlantic as early as 2000, the Germans persisted in believing him. In November 2002, according to Der Spiegel, Curveball's disclosures formed the centerpiece of a top secret briefing by the BND to the foreign affairs committee of the German parliament. One of those who were briefed to noted the "enormous discrepancy between the public statements made by the government" – which opposed the war and downplayed the Iraq threat – "and the knowledge it had in its possession."

Had Curveball's fabrications been exposed sooner, it would have prompted the Bush Administration to rely less on the WMD issue in its broader, and well-justified, case for the need to get rid of the Butcher of Baghdad.

As for Germany, it has yet to account for its own large contribution to the bad intelligence – intelligence it later pretended never to have believed in the first place. The Curveball shows that the intelligence failures regarding Iraq were world-wide and included many of those who would later become the war's fiercest critics.

Saddam's Weapons of Mass Destruction

George Piro, was the FBI agent who debriefed Saddam Hussein following his capture in December 2003. The Lebanese-born Piro, one of only a handful of agents at the bureau who speaks Arabic, was able to wheedle information from Saddam over a matter of months through a combination of flattery and ego-deflation that worked wonders with the former despot. The FBI interrogator says that, while Saddam said he no longer had active WMD programs in 2003, the dictator admitted that he intended to resume those programs as soon as he possibly could.

In a "60 minutes" interview, the relevant segment, appeared well down in the interview in typical Liberal bias:

Mr. Piro: "The folks that he needed to reconstitute his program are still there."
Mr. Pelley: "And that was his intention?"
Mr. Piro: "Yes."
Mr. Pelley: "What weapons of mass destruction did he intend to pursue again once he had the opportunity?"
Mr. Piro: "He wanted to pursue all of WMD. So he wanted to reconstitute his entire WMD program."
Mr. Pelley: "Chemical, biological, even nuclear."
Mr. Piro: "Yes."

Iraq's active WMD program had been destroyed, mostly by U.N. weapons inspectors, sometime in the 1990s, but Saddam told Mr. Piro that he maintained a pretense of having those weapons mainly to keep Iran at bay. Saddam's admission that an Iraqi WMD program remained a threat so long as Saddam remained in power cannot be lightly dismissed. Opponents of his ouster by military force argue that none of this matters because Saddam and his ambitions were being "contained" by U.N. sanctions. Hardly. As the Los Angeles Times reported in December 2000, "sanctions are crumbling among U.S. allies, who have begun challenging them with dozens of unauthorized flights into Iraq."

Bowing to this reality, the Bush Administration came to office the following month promising to ease the sanctions regime, even as it spent billions patrolling the so-called "No-Fly Zones." And as we learned after the invasion, Saddam was well on his way to breaking free of the sanctions by bribing everyone from a British member of parliament to a former French cabinet minister, all through a U.N. convenience known as Oil for Food.

In another telling moment in the "60 Minutes" interview, Mr. Piro relates that when he asked Saddam about his use of chemical weapons against Kurdish civilians, the dictator acknowledged that he had given the orders personally and explained himself in a word: "Necessary." The same applied for deposing Saddam.

CHAPTER 10
DEMOCRACY ABROAD
AND SECURITY AT
HOME

Liberals have killed Prospects for Democracy in Arabia

The Bush administration made democratization of the Middle East a strategic goal. Arab nations in the Middle East, largely led by monarchies and authoritarian governments, had made moves toward democracy. Now Arab rulers are emphasizing that change is a slow process. They realize that they can wait out the end of the Bush administration and have put the brakes on democratization.

In Egypt, the government of President Hosni Mubarak, which allowed a contested presidential election two years ago, has delayed municipal elections by two years.

In Jordan, King Abdullah II issued political change and democratization mandates. Now proponents see their hand weakened, with a document advocating change put on the back burner.

Parliamentary elections in Qatar have been postponed to 2007.

In Saudi Arabia, King Abdullah has refused requests that the country's consultative council be elected.

The Bush administration has been increasingly seen as weakened at home by Liberal attacks. Arab leaders are betting that the American public is losing its appetite for major interventions, giving them a freer hand. They remember Vietnam. They know that US Liberals have no staying power. What is more damaging is that Iran knows also. They know that in reality they have a free hand to do whatever they would like, particularly as newly released US expenditures are unacceptably high.

With the passage of the largest emergency spending bill in history, annual expenditures in Iraq have doubled since the U.S. commenced the Iraq Operation, as the military confronts the rapidly escalating cost of repairing, rebuilding and replacing equipment chewed up by three years of combat.

The cost has continued to rise, from $48 billion in 2003 to $59 billion in 2004 to $81 billion in 2005 to an anticipated $94 billion in 2006, according to the Center for Strategic and Budgetary Assessments. The U.S. government is now spending nearly $10 billion a month in Iraq and Afghanistan, up from $8.2 billion a year ago, a new Congressional Research Service report found. Annual war costs in Iraq are easily outpacing the $61 billion a year that the United States spent in Vietnam between 1964 and 1972, in today's dollars. The costs of the shock and awe high-tech laser-guided bombs, cruise missiles and stealth aircraft are now coming into focus as the military confronts equipment repair and rebuilding costs.

British tactics and underwhelming Force as perfected by Britain in Malaysia are a necessity if the only superpower is to be a superpower and show leadership in the world.

The American public has so far shown that it is not up to the task.

The Senate has passed a $109 billion bill to pay for the war in Iraq and hurricane aid for the Gulf Coast including an additional $14 billion of add-ons. It contains $65.7 billion for war operations and $28.8 billion for hurricane relief, including grants to states to build and repair housing and $3.9 billion for levees and flood control projects in Louisiana, plus such items as $4 billion in farm disaster aid, $1 billion in state grants and $1.1 billion in aid to the Gulf Coast seafood industry, which the President says he will not accept.

Conservative voters blame the White House and Congress for runaway government spending, illegal immigration and lack of action on social issues such as a constitutional amendment outlawing homosexual marriage. Those concerns come on top of public worries about Iraq and gasoline prices.

US Liberals have made the US less Secure

Spying is no longer an effective tool and as a consequence terrorist attacks on US soil will result. What is more important loss of innocent lives or loss of civil liberties of terrorist suspects?

The New York Times wiretapping exposé has ruined one of our most effective anti-al Qaeda surveillance programs. A federal judge has ordered the Justice Department to respond to requests by a civil liberties group for documents about President Bush's domestic eavesdropping program. The ruling was a victory for the Electronic Privacy Information Center, which sued the department under the Freedom of Information Act in seeking the release of the documents. U.S. District Judge Henry Kennedy ruled that the department must finish processing the group's requests and produce or identify all records.

Vice President Dick Cheney defended the Bush administration's domestic surveillance program, saying it is an essential tool in monitoring al-Qaeda and other terrorist organizations. But Cheney stressed that the program was limited and conducted in a way that safeguarded civil liberties.

The leaked Washington Post story on alleged prisons in Europe has done enormous damage to our ability to secure future cooperation in the war on terror from countries that don't want their assistance to be exposed.

Amnesty International has reported that prisoner abuse continues at facilities in Iraq maintained both by US forces and the Iraqi government. US authorities denied the allegations. An official of the Iraqi Interior Ministry also rejected the allegations. The Liberal media publicized this information widely. US Liberals beat the drum that at Guantanamo and in Iraq, the United States undermines its claim to the moral high ground when it does not hold itself and the new Iraq government to the highest human rights standards.

There are frequent instances of unseemly symbiosis between elements of the press corps and a cabal of partisan bureaucrats at the CIA who have been trying to undermine the Bush Presidency.

The existence of this intelligence insurgency first came to light in a major way with former Ambassador Joe Wilson, who wrote a New York Times op-ed in 2003 questioning the veracity of President Bush's "16 words" about Iraq seeking uranium in Africa. Someone close to the White House had the audacity to point out that Mr. Wilson was an anti-Bush partisan whose only claim to authority on the matter was the result of wifely nepotism. Mr. Wilson has since been thoroughly discredited, including in a bipartisan report from the Senate Intelligence Committee. But former Vice Presidential Chief of Staff Scooter Libby was prosecuted as the result of a media-instigated investigation into the "leak" of Valerie Plame's not-so-secret CIA identity.

These leaks are deeply troubling to all who truly care about democratic government. The CIA leakers are assuming the right to subvert the policy of our elected Administration.

Zacarias Moussaoui will live in solitary confinement for the rest of his life in a 7 feet by 11 feet soundproof, concrete cell without contact with anyone including speaking or make eye contact with other inmates at the Administrative Maximum United States Penitentiary south of Denver. He will be monitored 24 hours a day by surveillance cameras and will be shackled whenever removed from his cell. At best he will have a small black-and-white television with a limited number of channels. This is Liberal court sanctioned cruel and unusual punishment.

CHAPTER 11
ECONOMY/INCOME/
TAX

For Many, a Boom That Wasn't

The Fiscal Mess in the USA is a major reason for President Bush's unpopularity but its causes are principally outside his control. Nevertheless the USA and many Americans are not doing well and the President is blamed.

Over the last five years the overall economy grew every year often at a good pace. The now-finished boom was, for most Americans, nothing of the sort. In 2000, at the end of the previous economic expansion, the median American family made about $61,000, according to the Cencus Bureau's inflation-adjusted numbers. In 2007, in what looks to have been the final year of the most recent expansion, the median family made less — about $60,500.

A decline in incomes has never happened before, at least not for as long as the government has been keeping records. In every other expansion since World War II, the buying power of most American families grew while the economy did. In the second half of the 20th century, the USA became, became the richest country on earth. Now, though, most families aren't getting any richer.

The causes of the wage slowdown have been building for a long time. They have relatively little to do with President Bush or any other individual politician. The slowdown began in the 1970s, with an oil shock that raised the cost of everyday living. The technological revolution and the rise of global trade followed, reducing the bargaining power of a large section of the work force. In recent years, the cost of health care has aggravated the problem, by taking a huge bite out of most workers' paychecks.

Real median family income more than doubled from the late 1940s to the late '70s. It has risen less than 25 percent in the three decades since. The modern American economy then distributes the fruits of its growth to a relatively narrow slice of the population. Then came a technology bubble that made everything seem better, for a time. Record-low oil prices in the 1990s helped, too. So did the recent housing bubble, allowing families to supplement their incomes by taking equity out of their homes.

Now, though, we are out of bubbles.

The United States spends a great deal of money on education but has still lost its standing as the country with the highest college graduation rate in the world. (South Korea has passed us and Japan, Britain and Canada are close behind.) Many blacks in particular drop out of High School and an extraordinary number graduate to prison at huge cost to the rest of us. Many black girls in particular become single parent low income or non-earners costing tax payers dearly. Black racism is a major problem in the USA. Almost all will vote for Obama since he is their candidate; in fact he is biracial, abandoned by his black father, a not uncommon occurrence, largely brought up by his white grandparents in relative opulence in private schools in Hawaii after his 'flower child' white mother also had a brief marriage to an Indonesian and lived in a relatively poor Muslim environment in Indonesia, where Obama experienced intolerance towards what they considered to be an American black child.

Spending on physical infrastructure is at a 20-year high as a share of gross domestic product, but too much of the money is spent on the inefficient pork barrel programs championed by individual members of Congress to ensure their re-election. Congress is populated with second raters and their hangers-on, who are hopelessly corrupt.

Health care is considered to be an entitlement particularly by those who are less wealthy. Treatment options and associated costs are ever expanding but the only people who have their wherewithal to pay for everyone, are the wealthy, through increased taxation.

Our tax system has now become an inefficient tool to attempt to redistribute wealth with the most wealthy able to find loopholes and the burden falling on those who are upwardly mobile, reducing their motivation to stay in the earned income pool in the USA, as they see their hard work disproportionately benefiting those who contribute nothing but problems to our society. In 2005, the richest 1% paid about 39% of all income taxes. The richest 5% paid 60%, and the richest 10% paid 70%. These tax shares are all up substantially since 1990, and even somewhat since 2000. Meanwhile, Americans with an income below the median - half of all households - paid only 3% of all income taxes in 2005.

Income Inequality

The gap between rich and poor in many U.S. states has broadened at a quickening pace since the last recession, which could make it difficult for low-income families to weather the current economic downturn.

Since the late 1990s, average incomes have declined 2.5% for families on the bottom fifth of the country's economic ladder, while incomes have increased 9.1% for families on the top fifth. The result is that the average incomes of the top 5% of families are 12 times the average incomes of the bottom 20%. The top 1 percent of all income earners makes 20 percent of the total income. The top 1 percent of wealth holders has close to one-third of all wealth. The top 5 percent of wealth holders have 50 percent of all wealth in the USA.

Middle-class neighborhoods, long regarded as incubators for the American dream, are losing ground in cities across the country, shrinking at more than twice the rate of the middle class itself. In their place, poor and rich neighborhoods are both on the rise, as cities and suburbs have become increasingly segregated by income. As a share of all urban and suburban neighborhoods, middle-income neighborhoods in the nation's 100 largest metro areas have declined from 58 percent in 1970 to 41 percent in 2000. Since the late 1980s, income gaps widened in 37 states and have not narrowed in any states and the trend toward growing inequality has accelerated. The middle class has remained virtually stagnant, with average incomes growing just 1.3% in nearly eight years, according to U.S. Census Bureau data collected from 1987 through 2006. (It did not include capital gains and losses in its calculations.)

In Connecticut, incomes of the wealthiest 20% are eight times those of the poorest 20%. New York has the greatest disparity, with incomes of the top 20% 8.7 times the bottom ones, followed by Alabama, where the top are 8.5 times the bottom.

In Defense of Capitalism

Goldman Sachs's 2006 compensation numbers were staggering: $16.5 billion, up 40 percent in a year, some $623,000 per employee. Even with all-nighters and 24/7 work, Goldman employees probably earned the best hourly wages in the world (an average of about $200 per hour, assuming a 60-hour week; the firm's top traders, meanwhile, reportedly made $17,000 to $33,000 an hour.) In a country where some people are starving and others are furiously debating a $1 increase in the minimum wage, such bonanzas provide a startling reminder of the inequities of our free-market economy.

Within a more limited context, pay for performance compensation is fair. Capitalism works because it encourages and rewards those who successfully take risks, adapt to change and develop profitable opportunities. Goldman Sachs employees, arguably, are consistently better at those things than any other group of employees in the world. Yes, they have the good fortune of working in the right industry in a favorable market environment. But they have taken spectacular advantage of both.

In 2006, even after pay and other expenses, Goldman's employees generated an average of about $550,000 of pre-tax profit apiece. This is twice as much as the employees of Lehman Brothers, another strong Wall Street firm ($228,000). It is more than the employees at G.E. and Microsoft. It is even more than the employees at Google, another fantastically profitable wealth-generation machine.

Like workers at other Wall Street firms, most Goldman employees receive the vast majority of their compensation in a single paycheck, the amount of which is based on firm, group and individual performance. This annual bonus system mirrors the dynamics of free-market capitalism.

The system gives the firm extraordinary ability to invest its resources in the assets (people) that earn the biggest returns — and to do so without risk, after the fact, when the returns are in the bank. It allows the firm to pay superstars enough that they won't jump to other companies. The bonus system also gives the firm the flexibility to cut compensation drastically in bad years without destroying profit margins or firing thousands of loyal employees. Wall Street is notoriously cyclical. The system ensures that ambitious employees have an incentive to give their best every year, instead of resting on laurels.

Capitalism encourages successful risk-taking, which keeps our economy healthy and vibrant. Capitalism is also great at generating immense tax revenue (Goldman's employees pump almost as much into city, state and government coffers as they take home.

CEO Compensation

In 2004, the average top executive at a big company earned 170 times the average worker's pay. These executives receive a combination of salaries, bonuses and stock grants. And their perks can even include infusions of cash to offset the taxes everyone else is expected to pay.

When firms that promise to do objective financial statements also attempt to woo the client it is auditing into other kinds of deals, the temptations are obvious. To make the decisions on executive pay, many companies create compensation committees, drawn from the board of directors. That committee in turn is advised by outside consultants, experts in how much others in the field are getting paid.

The outside consultants who advise Verizon, Hewitt Associates, do considerable other business for the company. Hewitt operates Verizon's employee benefits Web sites and performs actuarial work for three of the company's pension plans. The company has racked up more than half a billion dollars in revenue from Verizon and its predecessors since

1997. The end result is predictable. Verizon CEO Seidenberg received a package worth $19.4 million last year, as his shareholders felt the pinch of a stock that fell 26 percent.

Top executives are snatching more than their fair share of corporate proceeds and the board of directors is not performing its function as internal guardian of the company's health.

Executive excess makes good copy. Enron's Ken Lay made $233 million over three years and owned six vacation homes when Enron declared bankruptcy in 2001.

Most CEOs have better ethics, but don't shun material benefits. Exxon chairman Lee Raymond is retiring with a package worth nearly $400 million. Leaders of the top 500 US companies each made $11.7 million on average last year. And the gap with regular workers has widened enormously. CEOs who made 42 times an average worker's pay in 1980, now collect more than 10 times that, according to Business Week.

Big bucks make big headlines, but the more important story is what is happening at the lower end of the income gap. Real average wages have risen only about 1 percent per year for more than two decades. A study of US trends by the National Academies in Washington concluded: "For the first time in generations, the nation's children could face poorer prospects than their parents and grandparents did."

Wealth Creation

Wide scale wealth creation occurs when succeeding generations stand on the shoulders of the previous generation

New business flounders because people are more concerned about dividing the pot before there is a pot. A difficulty in new business development is that people want to be paid in hard cash when there is no cash generation. There is a reluctance to provide sweat equity. Where the culture is to take and not to give, there is no action.

Risk taking requires an acceptance of mistakes and failure. It is important to celebrate mistakes so that we learn from them. That is the ultimate education. You only learn to win after you have learned to lose.

If you are not moving ahead you are moving backwards – relatively and frequently literally.

Taxes and Income

Every Liberal Politician wants to raise taxes on "the rich," but they will have to work hard to out tax President Bush. No Administration in modern history has done more to pry tax revenue from the wealthy.

In 2005, the richest 1% paid about 39% of all income taxes. The richest 5% paid 60%, and the richest 10% paid 70%. These tax shares are all up substantially since 1990, and even somewhat since 2000. Meanwhile, Americans with an income below the median -- half of all households -- paid only 3% of all income taxes in 2005. The richest 1% (1.3 million) had adjusted gross incomes of more than $365,000 in 2005. They paid ten times more income tax than all of the 66 million American tax filers below the median in income.

For Liberals and most of the media, these facts mean only that the rich are getting richer, so of course they're paying more taxes. It is true that the top earners have increased their share of total income. Yet, the rich showed more rapid gains in reported income shares in the 1990s than in the first half of this decade. The share of the richest 1% jumped to 20.8% of total income in 2000, from 14% in 1990, but increased only slightly to 21.2% in 2005. It is not true that "rising inequality" resulted from the Bush tax cuts. The Clinton years were far worse for "inequality."

Indeed, the share of taxes paid by the top 1% has kept climbing this decade -- to 39.4% in 2005, from 37.4% in 2000. The share paid by the top 5% has increased even more rapidly. In other words, despite the tax reductions of 2001 and 2003, the rich saw their share of taxes paid rise at a faster rate than their share of income.

One explanation is that the Bush tax cuts reduced the income tax liability of middle and lower income households by more proportionately than the rich. The average family of four with an income of $40,000 saw its income tax liability fall by about $2,052 a year from the 2001 and 2003 tax cuts.

Also the USA continues to be a society of upward income mobility. Over the past decade, millions of Americans have joined the once highly exclusive club of six- and seven-figure earners. Some 304,000 Americans earned $1 million or more in annual income in 2005, compared to 110,000 in 1996 and 176,000 in 2000. The number of millionaire households in net worth also increased to nine million in 2006, up from six million in 2001. More than 13 million American households, or about one in 10, had an income of more than $100,000 a year in 2005.

The IRS only records the income that taxpayers report. Its data don't include income that the rich hide in tax shelters or otherwise defer. Lower tax rates since 1981 have caused the rich to declare more of what they earn. In 1980, when the top income tax rate was 70%, the richest 1% paid only 19% of all income taxes; now, with a top rate of 35%, they pay more than double that share. With lower rates and fewer tax loopholes after President Reagan's 1986 reform, there is less incentive to shelter income to avoid tax.

IRS figures include income that makes many Americans rich only for a single year. In 2005, for example, taxpayers earned an estimated $600 billion in income from capital gains, which is reported on tax forms as part of adjustable gross income. That includes the one-time gain from retirees that has lived modestly for decades when they sell the family business or home for $1 million or more. They are benefiting in one year from a lifetime of hard work and thrift.

The amount of capital gains declared on tax forms has doubled since the tax rate was cut to 15% from 20% in 2003, which has also contributed to more Americans being "rich." Dividend income has also increased by at least 50% since that rate was cut to 15% from nearly 40% in 2003. So part of the income gains of the rich are simply a result of assets that have been converted into taxable income to take advantage of lower tax rates.

Liberals should try to understand that the best way to soak the rich is to lower tax rates.

Clintons' Taxes

New York Senator Hillary Clinton and her husband spend a lot of time on the Presidential trail deploring the "wealthy" and "well-connected." As their newly released tax records for 2000 to 2007 show, they know of whom they speak.

The Clinton's income was $109 million over the past eight years, putting them among the top .01% of taxpayers. Most of the Clintons' income came from speech-making ($51.9 million) and book-writing ($29.6 million), as they cash in on the Presidency.

Their political status has given them access to wealthy people who have made them rich. That is why they took so long to release their returns, and why they are still reluctant to release additional information. Bill Clinton raked $15 million as an adviser and rainmaker for billionaire financier Ron Burkle's Yucaipa firm. The former President also took in $3.3 million in consulting fees from InfoUSA CEO Vinod Gupta, who has also helped fund Mrs. Clinton's White House bid.

The Clintons have claimed $10.2 million in charitable giving over these eight years as a deduction against income to reduce their taxable income. Nearly all the donations went to the Clinton Family Foundation, which has disbursed only half the money. The Clintons use the foundation for 'strategic giving', such as the $100,000 it donated last year to a local South Carolina library – the day after Mrs. Clinton debated in that key primary state. Most of the foundation's disbursements came only after Mrs. Clinton announced her Presidential run.

Similar conflict-of-interest questions apply to the separate William Jefferson Clinton Foundation, for which the couple has so far refused to release a list of donors. One donor is Canadian mining tycoon Frank Giustra, who took Mr. Clinton along on a trip to Kazakhstan as a character reference, won a Kazakh mining concession, and gave more than $30 million to the foundation.

The Clintons should understand the unnecessary complexity of the tax code. Their 2006 return alone totaled 67 pages. While they can afford the smartest accountants to wend there way through all those forms, Mrs. Clinton is not promoting tax reform. Her main tax proposal is to repeal the tax cuts of 2001 and 2003, raising rates to the levels of the Clinton Presidency. "We didn't ask for George Bush's tax cuts. We didn't want them, and we didn't need them," Mrs. Clinton explained. Now we know why.

Her higher tax rates will soak middle-class families that make $100,000 or $200,000 a year and hardly feel 'rich'. The Clinton's advisors know how to avoid taxes. Once Hillary pulls the plug on her bid for the Presidency, the Clinton's tax avoidance strategies will become much more aggressive. After all, Hillary made $100,000 overnight from commodity trades from nothing and no knowledge. Tax avoidance will be easy for the Clintons and their Liberal beliefs will not stand in the way.

One for George Bush

A steep rise in tax revenues from corporations and the wealthy is driving down the budget deficit this year, even though spending has climbed sharply because of the war in Iraq and the cost of hurricane relief. Tax receipts will be about $250 billion above last year's levels and the deficit will be about $100 billion less than projected six months ago.

The rising tide in tax payments has been building for months. Tax revenues are climbing so fast that the budget deficit will decline this year. The main reason is a big spike in corporate tax receipts, which have nearly tripled since 2003, as well as a big increase in individual taxes on stock market profits and executive bonuses.

The Congressional Budget Office reported that corporate tax receipts for the nine months ending in June, 2007 hit $250 billion — nearly 26 percent higher than the same time last year — and that overall revenues were $206 billion higher than at this point in 2005. The deficit this year will shrink to less than $300 billion, from $318 billion in 2005 and an all-time high of $412 billion in 2004.

"The tax relief we delivered has helped unleash the entrepreneurial spirit of America and kept our economy the envy of the world," President Bush said.

The revenue jump vindicates the Republican tax cuts, especially the 2003 tax cut on stock dividends. As promised, the tax cuts have spurred the economy and increased revenues. Could it be that George Bush knows what he is doing and is right on this issue – and others?

Entrepreneurial Capitalism

Former Fed chief Alan Greenspan's optimism for our U.S. economy rests on one word: innovation. Robert Litan, Vice President of Research and Policy at the entrepreneurship-oriented Kauffman Foundation elaborates in some detail in his recent book, "Good Capitalism, Bad Capitalism and the Economics of Growth and Prosperity," on how the U.S. has come to be the beacon of "entrepreneurial capitalism." And it is this very entrepreneurial capitalism that has produced, and may likely continue to produce, the innovation Greenspan is counting on.

Entrepreneurial capitalism is the successor to managerial, bureaucratic or "big firm" capitalism. Further, it is this, and only this form of capitalism that can provide sustained economic growth by continuing to provide the fuel (innovation) necessary to ignite such growth. Litan notes that, with the exception of the transistor (invented by Bell Labs) and the hybrid car (commercialized by Honda and Toyota), all major radical innovations of the last 100 years have come from an entrepreneur. Litan posits it is this entrepreneurial radical innovation that has led, and can continue to lead, to big surges in productivity growth.

How did we get here by moving away from Big Steel, Big Oil, Ma Bell and their ilk? A major force has been the doubling of computer power every 24 months or so. All of us have been freed from the need for big bureaucracy to create this acceleration in computing power. With this personal power, we have benefited from a myriad of new software tools. Most of us turn to computers to read e-mails, watch some shows, play fantasy football, etc., but there are just enough technology entrepreneurs who have the itch to tease out a revolutionary idea or follow a dream.

Quotes of Note

Dreaming, planning and goal-setting are the building blocks of entrepreneurial success.

"You see things; and you say, 'Why?' But I dream things that never were; and I say, 'Why not?'"
George Bernard Shaw

"What is not started today is never finished tomorrow."
Johann Wolfgang von Goethe

"Success is not final, failure is not fatal: it is the courage to continue that counts"
Winston Churchill

"Really great people make you feel that you, too, can become great."
Mark Twain

"Goals are dreams with deadlines."
Diana Scharf Hunt

Kiva.org.

Kiva is the world's first person-to-person micro-lending website, empowering individuals to lend directly to an entrepreneur in the developing world. Kiva will have facilitated loans totaling $100 million by 2010. Learn more about this phenomenal organization and idea at www.kiva.org.

Private Equity

The initials "PE" have morphed from "private equity" into "public enemy." Attacks from politicians about carried interest grew into broader attacks in newspapers and on the airwaves by those who have felt that, somehow, private equity adds nothing to the wealth of nations, but rather to the superwealth of the captains and shipmates of these firms.

Now, it appears, such shouts from U.S. shores are echoing back even more loudly from overseas. Witness a commentary in Le Monde Diplomatique by Senior Editor Ignacio Ramonet titled, "Private equity is on the prowl." In this diatribe, private equity companies (mainly of the American variety) are depicted as "the new vultures .... predatory investment funds with vast amounts of capital" engaged in a "brutal form of capitalism."

Ramonet asserts that PE firms are taking over the global economy, and that they cannot be stopped! He writes, "One American in four, and almost one Frenchman or woman in 12, now works for them." His asserts that PE firms in the U.S. and Britain acquired 400 companies in France last year for $14 billion. His disdain for private equity is clear in his declarations that "[their] idea is to get round the fundamental principles of capitalist morality and back to the law of the jungle." He ends his piece, "Some thought that, with the advent of globalization, capital was sated. It is now clear that there is no end to its greed."

Wow! We know that the French are more left-leaning than their American brethren, but such a scathing attack in such a prominent weekly gives me pause. I am not sure many partners in firms had imagined themselves as the robber barons they are being painted by Ramonet. Our only option is to shrug and say, "Chacun à son gout"

How Foreclosures Will Change the Presidential Election

"The thinking it took to get us into this mess is not the same thinking that is going to get us out of it." Albert Einstein.

We have red states, we have blue states and increasingly we have purple states, beat-up states with substantial and growing numbers of foreclosures, states that may well decide the next presidential election.

The foreclosure issue is being politicized because it's too big to ignore and too many people are being impacted. Foreclosures are an emerging issue because they lead to reduced local home values and home values are one of the key measures of personal success. Foreclosures are front-page news, they're affecting financial markets worldwide and for the first time in decades the lending system, foreclosure practices and bankruptcy rules may all be changed.

The political system is set up to assure that both large and small states are well-represented in Washington. Every state has two senators as well as a congressional delegation related to population size. By themselves, the top ten foreclosure states represent 20 of the 100 senate seats as well as 183 of the 435 members of the House of Representatives (42 percent).

The foreclosure states will play a pivotal role in the upcoming presidential election. In the U.S. we do not elect presidents by direct popular vote; instead we have an "electoral college" of one elector for each house and senate seat plus three for the District of Columbia, a total of 538.

To control the U.S. government you need 51 senators, 218 house members and 270 electoral votes. The number of house, senate and electoral seats represented by the 10 top foreclosure states are not enough, by themselves, to gain control of the government. But any candidate or party that wins the purple states will also win the next presidential election. Here's why:

In terms of the presidency, the purple states represent 203 of the 270 electoral votes needed for victory. Seen the other way, of the 335 electoral votes outside the purple zone a candidate would need to capture just 67 votes to win the presidency — one-fifth of all other electoral votes. This could be done with victories in few as 13 states, the 10 purple jurisdictions plus New York (31 electoral votes), Illinois (21) and Pennsylvania (also 21).

A winning presidential campaign does not guarantee a house or senate majority but it surely helps those affiliated with a winning national ticket. The Founders shrewdly engineered a system where the states needed to win the presidency and the houses are insufficient by themselves to control the senate. It's entirely possible for one party to win the presidency and lose one or both houses of Congress.

How Much Disclosure Is Enough?

It's hardly a secret that few borrowers fully understand their mortgage options. A 2006 Federal Reserve study found that 20 percent of all ARM borrowers did not know their original loan rate and 35 percent had no idea how much their monthly payment could increase with each adjustment. Amazingly, 41 percent didn't even know the maximum interest rate for their loans.

In a 2007 study, the Federal Trade Commission came to similar conclusions:

Current mortgage cost disclosures failed to convey key mortgage costs to many consumers.

Both prime and sub prime borrowers failed to understand key loan terms when viewing the current disclosures, and both benefited from improved disclosures.

Improved disclosures provided the greatest benefit for more complex loans, where both prime and sub prime borrowers had the most difficulty understanding loan terms.

As these surveys show, disclosure requirements for real estate financing have plainly been inadequate. If large numbers of borrowers are not aware of basic loan costs, one can only imagine what they've missed in terms of prepayment penalties, lender fees and hidden charges.

The assumption regarding taxes and insurance — an assumption used for both the fixed-rate and adjustable-rate loan products — raises a question: Of the millions of homes in the US, how many have had unchanged tax and insurance costs during the past five years? Rising governmental costs assure increased property taxes while insurance rates in many states have soared in recent years because of hurricanes, floods and other hazards. The property tax and insurance assumptions made within the chart are inherently unrealistic, do not disclose the real-world likelihood of rising taxes and growing insurance costs and therefore understate potential costs.

New Bankruptcy Laws Spur Foreclosures

Almost 30 years have passed since the Bankruptcy Reform Act of 1978, a time when mortgages typically had a fixed-rate and unchanging monthly costs. Back then — and until 2005 — if you ran into financial trouble bankruptcy provided a way out and a fresh start.

In 2005 declaring bankruptcy — something that was never simple, easy or pleasant to begin with — became far tougher. Under the Bankruptcy Abuse Prevention and Consumer Protection Act creditors suddenly had new protections — and borrowers didn't.

What changed? Most student loans can no longer be discharged. If your income exceeds the state medium you can be forced to file under Chapter 13 (a repayment program) and not Chapter 7 (a discharge and forgiveness plan). Credit debt is not forgiven if you spend at least $500 in the 60 days prior to seeking bankruptcy protection -- say a cash advance to pay off a looming mortgage payment. Perhaps most importantly for mortgage borrowers, the 2005 legislation says homeowners must obtain credit counseling and develop a budget analysis in the 180-day period before filing for bankruptcy.

If you put all the changes together the results are predictable: Bankruptcy filings should fall and that's exactly what happened. According to court filings there were 1,597,462 bankruptcies in 2004 and 2,078,415 bankruptcies in 2005. As for 2006, bankruptcies declined 70 percent to 617,660 cases.

The falling number of bankruptcies and the rising numbers of foreclosures are related. In basic terms, under the old bankruptcy rules it was often possible to delay a foreclosure action by stalling the creditor in court and using that time to sell or refinance the property.

The 1978 legislation had an unusual mortgage-related requirement. It provided that while a bankruptcy court could modify and adjust various debts, including the mortgage on a vacation home, it could not modify the mortgage on a prime residence. A literal interpretation of this language was upheld in 1993 by the Supreme Court in its Nobleman decision.

The practical effect of the current bankruptcy law is that borrowers stuck in unaffordable home loans must cure their defaults and, in addition, make monthly payments on the loans according to their terms or lose their homes.

The Budget of a Lame-duck President

President George W. Bush's 2009 budget is a tour through his priorities, failed fiscal policies and the legacy that he will leave for the next president. With President Bush on his way out, it is not clear how many of the President's priorities, will survive. Among its many aspects, the budget includes billions more for a defense against ballistic missiles that shows no signs of working. What will definitely outlast President Bush for years to come are big deficits.

The President states that his plan will put the country on the path to balancing the budget by 2012. His proposal projects a $410 billion deficit for 2008 and a $407 billion deficit next year. President Bush's projection for a balanced budget in 2012 assumes only partial funding for the wars in Iraq and Afghanistan for 2009, and no such spending - zero - starting in 2010. It also assumes that there will be no long-running relief from the alternative minimum tax and that there will be deep cuts in Medicare and other health care spending that have proved to be politically impossible to enact.

The big expense is the Pentagon. After adjusting for inflation, the proposed defense budget of $515.4 billion - which does not include either war spending or the cost of nuclear weapons - would be up by more than 30 percent since President Bush took office and would be the highest level of military spending since World War II.

President Bush's military involvement in Iraq, on top of Afghanistan, has seriously strained the American military. The new president will keep asking for large Pentagon budgets, both to rebuild military equipment and to prepare the country to face what will continue to be a very dangerous world.

There is a continuing lack of fiscal restraint in Washington. Not a single weapons system will be canceled. Congress - far too captive to military-industry lobbyists – will also not scale back or cancel expensive programs that don't meet today's threats, or tomorrow's.

Budget Excesses

On December 19th, 2007, the Democratic Congress passed a 3,400-page, $516 billion "omnibus" budget bill which President Bush is prepared to sign. Mr. Bush has used his veto power to back Congress down from its typical excesses. The good news is that Democrats conceded to Mr. Bush's spending cap of $933 billion in domestic discretionary spending for 2008 -- or $22 billion less than Democrats proposed in their spring budget resolution. Over five years, that $22 billion will save about $205 billion because it won't become part of the annual "baseline" that the politicians use as a starting point for next year's automatic budget increases. This victory is modest but real.

Democrats also agreed to strip the bill of numerous policy changes that Mr. Bush had threatened to veto. Gone are limits on union disclosure reports. Gone, too, is an expansion of demands to pay prevailing union wages even on non-union work sites; as well as an easing of the Cuban trade embargo. Congress is also funding the wars in Iraq and Afghanistan to the tune of $70 billion - something Democratic leaders had vowed not to do.

When combined with the Defense spending bill that has already been signed, Congress will still exceed Mr. Bush's $933 billion "top-line" thanks to about $11 billion in budget gimmicks and "emergency" spending. This includes $2.9 billion for "border security," $100 million for security for the Democratic and Republican conventions next year, $500 million for California wildfires, plus more for home heating oil and other political favorites.

Even worse is the President's abdication on earmarks, or Member-requested pork. Mr. Bush had publicly insisted that Congress should cut the number of earmarks by 50% this year, from 13,492 in fiscal 2007. The "omnibus" includes 8,983 earmarks, which brings the total so far to 11,144 including those passed as part of the Defense bill. As a percentage decline that is only 17%.

The pork barrel includes $700 million for a Minnesota bike trail, $113,000 for rodent control in Alaska, and $1 million for an energy project in the district of Louisiana Democrat William Jefferson, who faces trial for bribery next year. Dozens of these earmarks were added into the bill at the last minute, when fiscal conservative Members lacked the time to find and fight them on the House or Senate floor.

Mr. Bush could have used these projects as his reason for vetoing the bill. Congress would then have had little choice but to pass a "continuing resolution" that maintained spending for 2008 at levels similar to this year. That would have been a true taxpayer triumph, and would have done far more to rehabilitate Mr. Bush's record on fiscal issues than this omnibus will.

House Republicans voted against the omnibus bill en masse. Democrats have shown that their claims of "fiscal discipline" are entirely phony.

Pay Soars in the Boardroom

Many corporate directors saw double-digit raises boost six-figure salaries last year, and the largess rolls on. That's for perhaps 12 meetings a year -- attendance optional.

Corporate directors at S&P 500 companies got hefty 20% pay hikes in 2005. The median pay for those directors was $139,000.

Directors argue higher pay makes sense because regulators and lawyers for shareholders are making boards more accountable for what happens inside companies. The truth is that boards are merely being asked to do what they were supposed to be doing all along: keeping an eye on the company for investors.

Many board members award themselves gold-plated pay packages even though they regularly play hooky in ways that would get the average worker canned in a heartbeat. More than 520 directors from 4,000 companies missed 25% or more of their board meetings in the last two years. Most of those meetings last just two days.

Nabors Industries paid director Hans Schmidt more than $1.2 million for his services as a director in 2004. Even so, Schmidt made only 70% of the energy drilling and exploration company's board meetings last year.

Despite Schmidt's attendance record, Nabors paid him an annual retainer worth $50,000 and granted him 43,000 stock options with a strike price of $45.91. Those options had a theoretical valuation of $1.25 million when granted, according to a common model for valuing options called Black-Scholes. With Nabors' stock trading recently at $76, the options had a real value of nearly $1.3 million to Schmidt, though he has to wait two years to cash in two-thirds of that 2004 options package.

Directors need sophisticated business management skills, the companies say. The board helps management plot strategy and is responsible for hiring -- and firing -- the CEO. Directors oversee financial reporting -- one of the many tasks that has become more difficult because of the Sarbanes-Oxley reforms and new standards put in place by stock exchanges following the post-tech bubble business scandals.

US Unemployed

Millions of men in the prime of their lives, between 30 and 55 — have dropped out of regular work. They are turning down jobs they think beneath them or are unable to find work for which they are qualified, even as an expanding economy offers opportunities to work.

About 13 percent of American men in this age group are not working, up from 5 percent in the late 1960's. The difference represents 4 million men who would be working today if the employment rate had remained where it was in the 1950's and 60's.

Most are former blue-collar workers with no more than a high school education. But their ranks are growing at all education and income levels. Refugees of failed Internet businesses have spent years out of work during their 30's, while former managers in their late 40's are trying to stretch severance packages and savings all the way to retirement.

Many of these men could find work if they had to, but with lower pay and fewer benefits than they once earned, and they have decided they prefer the alternative. It is a significant cultural shift from three decades ago, when men almost invariably went back into the work force after losing a job and were more often able to find a new one that met their needs.

The fastest growing source of help is a patchwork system of government support, the main one being federal disability insurance, which is financed by Social Security payroll taxes. The disability stipends range up to $1,000 a month and, after the first two years, Medicare kicks in, giving access to health insurance that for many missing men no longer comes with the low-wage jobs available to them.

No federal entitlement program is growing as quickly, with more than 6.5 million men and women now receiving monthly disability payments, up from 3 million in 1990. About 25 percent of the missing men are collecting this insurance. The ailments that qualify them are usually real, like back pain, heart trouble or mental illness. But in some cases, the illnesses are not so serious that they would prevent people from working if a well-paying job with benefits were an option.

The disability program, in turn, is an obstacle to working again. Taking a job holds the risk of demonstrating that one can earn a living and is thus no longer entitled to the monthly payments. But staying out of work has consequences. Skills deteriorate, along with the desire for a paying job and the habits that it requires.

Reaganomics

In the USA Reagan's pro-growth, tax cutting philosophy is in full-scale retreat: This Congress has proposed higher tax rates on personal income, capital gains and dividends. Ironically, the Reagan economic philosophy of lower taxes, less regulation and free trade has never been more in vogue abroad -- so much so that it has become the global economic operating system.

In the Pacific Rim nations, for example, Malaysia, New Zealand, Singapore, Taiwan and Vietnam all have cut taxes this year or have plans to do so. Singapore has cut taxes multiple times in recent years and it now operates with no capital gains tax.

But the remarkable attitudinal shift on taxes has been in Europe, which in the 1980s and '90s showcased their gold-plated social safety nets, boasted of their citizens' willingness to pay high tax rates to maintain them and was openly contemptuous of the Reagan tax-cutting philosophy. Now those same nations of old-Europe seem to be in a sprint to see which country can get their tax rates lowest quickest.

French President Nicolas Sarkozy has plans to cut his country's business income tax by at least five percentage points as part of his economic rehabilitation plan. Spain and Italy are negotiating plans to lower their corporate tax rates, and the U.K. already did so earlier this year. Sweden and Russia last year eliminated their estate taxes because they said the tax was economically counterproductive. In Germany under Chancellor Angela Merkel, the corporate tax rate has been reduced to less than 30% from 39%.

Some of this tax chopping in Old Europe is a response to the success of the U.S. tax rate reductions and the fast pace of job creation that ensued from economic growth. A bigger factor more recently has been the impact of the flat-tax revolution in Eastern Europe. There are now 14 nations with flat taxes, 10 of them in nations formerly behind the Iron Curtain.

Austria cut its corporate tax rate to keep pace with its neighbor, Slovakia which recently adopted an 18% flat tax. Singapore is cutting taxes to compete with its 16% flat-tax rival Hong Kong. Northern Ireland wants to cut its tax rates so that it can compete with the economic gazelle of Europe, the Republic of Ireland. In 1988 Ireland was a high-unemployment stagnant economy with a 48% corporate tax rate, today that rate is 12.5% and the rest of the world is now desperate to match its economic results.

The idea that jobs, businesses and wealth follow low tax rates is widely accepted. Nguyen Van Ninh, head of the Department of Taxation in Vietnam is typical. He concedes that the corporate tax cuts may lose revenues, but "on the other side, the business environment will become more and more attractive, resulting in increased investment."

This is all very good news -- except in the U.S. Arthur Laffer, one of the architects of the Reagan tax policies, believes that one major explanation for the strength of the euro and the weakness of the dollar in recent years is the divergent paths on tax policies on the two sides of the Atlantic. Europe is cutting levies, while the only debate among the political class in Washington is how high to jack them up.

Still, it is a testament to the Reagan economic revolution launched in 1981 that, a quarter century later, global tax rates are 25 percentage points lower on average today than in the 1970s. And those figures don't even include this latest round of chopping under Reaganomics. The enactment of supply-side policies is helping ignite one of the strongest and longest world-wide economic expansions in history.

The Democratic leadership in Congress believes that tax rates don't matter much if at all, and that the Bush tax cuts were a giveaway to the rich. John Edwards has even suggested a near doubling of the U.S. capital gains tax rate as part of his economic program, and his rivals all have schemes to soak the wealthy as well.

The USA is moving from leader to laggard in the global race for job creation, capital investment and prosperity.

The Pathetic US Dollar

Dollar weakness is neutralizing the positive effects of the Federal Reserve's interest-rate cuts. As the dollar spirals downward, weakened by Washington's indifference and market expectations of more rate cuts, liquidity drains from the U.S. into inflation hedges like gold and, in the case of entrepreneurship and risk-taking capital, to countries with strengthening currencies. This drain undercuts the growth impact of the Fed's recent rate cuts, complicating the recovery from the August credit-market turbulence.

Foreign countries are suffering the opposite phenomenon. Global investors want to buy more in strong-currency countries, heating up those countries' economies, land values and stock markets. If their central banks hike rates, as China has been doing and Australia did recently, it invites even more capital inflows in search of higher yields and currency appreciation, reinforcing the upward currency spiral.

Europeans, Canadians and others revel in their wealth relative to Americans. It's their chance to grow their risking-taking capital base, set global standards, and begin to dominate geopolitical issues.

The US should stop the currency rollercoaster. It is not clear why the US wants a super-weak dollar, driving innovation away from the U.S. and enriching our competitors.

Currency momentum can be broken. The dollar wouldn't be hard to strengthen if the Treasury included dollar weakness in G-7 discussions, and the Fed singled out dollar weakness as a concern.

The Fed is in a good position if it wants to strengthen the dollar. By cutting rates well before economic weakness, it has room to express stronger interest in the dollar's recovery even if that comes across as hawkish. A clearer preference for dollar strength would increase the demand for dollars, breaking the weak-dollar momentum without requiring currency intervention or rate hikes. As the dollar strengthens, capital would return to the U.S., providing extra liquidity and making the Fed's stimulus job easier.

The market's view is that the Fed has been proactive in providing liquidity but less so in creating conditions to keep it in the U.S. With gold topping $830 per ounce and the once-meek euro now weighing in at $1.47, it's simply not clear whether the Fed envisions any bounds to the dollar's slide.

Adding to the dollar's latest sell-off, the G-7 statement said the group's finance ministers "reaffirm that exchange rates should reflect economic fundamentals." Rather than "reflecting economic fundamentals," which are code words for the acceptance of instability, currencies should be "strong and stable" in order to create good fundamentals for private-sector growth.

The market's clear reaction to Washington's reliance on "fundamentals" has been to sell the dollar on the view that U.S. economic fundamentals are bad and getting worse. The communiqué pointedly left out any confidence-building phrases -- like the one in the 1992 G-7 statements that "the ministers and central bank governors . . . will take appropriate additional actions as needed to achieve sustained growth and greater currency stability."

Some argue that dollar weakness helps the economy by making our goods, workers and houses cheap enough for foreigners to buy or hire. This hasn't worked in practice because investors are momentum oriented -- they want assets that are going up, not down. The weaker the dollar in recent years, the more quickly capital has flowed out to emerging markets, commodities and foreign real estate. Cheap is assumed to become cheaper when a currency is weakening.

While the U.S. trade deficit has declined over the last year, most of that reflects the U.S. housing bust -- home-building is import-intensive -- and the foreign economic boom. The trade deficit is likely to remain wide regardless of the dollar's value. It reflects a huge demographic differential -- our major trading partners are aging much faster than we are, requiring them to save more while building and importing less.

Prolonged dollar weakness creates a multitude of problems. Companies have to devote an increasing portion of their time and energy to currencies rather than their operating business. Foreigners, not always friends, are gaining wealth relative to Americans. Rather than making the U.S. more competitive, the dollar's weakness makes it harder to justify investments in the U.S., where growth is slowing and interest rates are higher than in Europe or Japan to compensate for the weakening dollar. The investment killer is that assets in the U.S. keep losing value in foreign-currency terms, so U.S. opportunities have to be significantly better to entice investment in the face of a weakening dollar.

This doesn't mean the Fed was wrong in its Sept. 18 and Oct. 31 interest-rate cuts. By 2007, the Fed probably didn't have the option of undoing its 2003-2005 mistake of keeping interest rates too low too long -- the inexplicable "measured" hikes from a 1% interest rate during a U.S. and global boom. The damage in terms of dollar weakness, the housing bubble and credit market distortions was substantial, and the Fed's rate-cutting action appropriately lowered the recession risk.

The goal now should be to create the best future environment for growth. Alan Greenspan's new book conveys a long-term pessimism about the value of the dollar in an entitlement-heavy society. That should be addressed. The remedy is clear -- a new "strong and stable" dollar policy, personal accounts for Social Security, productivity improvements in medical care, and confidence in low future tax rates to restore growth and invite investments in dollar-denominated assets. None of these changes are likely with Liberals in control.

Values

You may wish that you had more material possessions. Real value comes from your relationships with others and the sense of pride you get from doing a job well. New possessions may lift your spirits, but it is a superficial elevation. Live modestly. Enough in the bank is all you need. More does not give happiness.

In our Liberal Society, values have become increasingly displaced but George Bush is not the right target. A free handout mentality, the expectation of something for nothing, a declining work ethic and a lowering of our moral compass are of increasing concern. We should look at ourselves for the causes of our dissatisfaction because we currently live in the best country on earth.

The "rich life" of popular imagination is no great shakes. People dream of endless leisure and bountiful possessions. Unfortunately, after a few months, endless leisure often seems like endless tedium. Similarly, you might imagine that a flashy new car or a fancy new home will be your ticket to eternal bliss. But a year after you make your purchase, the thrill will likely be gone, and you will be lusting after something else.

That doesn't mean money can't enhance your life. Wealth, or more importantly the ability to control one's expenditures to live within one's means, delivers three key benefits:

1. If you have money, you don't have to worry about it.

The feeling of financial serenity isn't only for the wealthy. If you live beneath your means and invest prudently, you can achieve a sense of financial control long before you achieve full financial independence.

2. Money can give you the freedom to pursue your passions.

You want to spend your days engaged in activities that you find absorbing and satisfying, that you feel you're good at -- and where you feel you're doing something of value.

Find work that you are passionate about and that allows you to mix pleasure and work. Pleasure can come from the opportunity to travel as you want and where you want.

You don't need to be financially independent to have a sense of purpose. You can pick a career that is close to your heart.

3. Money can buy you time with family and friends.

Seeing family and friends can provide a huge boost to happiness. Forget spending more money at the mall -- and instead spend more time with family and friends.

CHAPTER 12

ENVIRONMENT AND

POLITICS

Global Warming

The Opposing Point of View

MIT's Alfred P. Sloan professor of meteorology Richard Lindzen has complained about the 'shrill alarmism of Al Gore's movie "An Inconvenient Truth." Lindzen acknowledges that global warming is real, and he acknowledges that increased carbon emissions might be causing the warming -- but they also might not.

"We do not understand the natural internal variability of climate change" is one of Lindzen's many heresies, along with such zingers as "the Arctic was as warm or warmer in 1940," "the evidence so far suggests that the Greenland ice sheet is actually growing on average," and "Alpine glaciers have been retreating since the early 19th century, and were advancing for several centuries before that. Since about 1970, many of the glaciers have stopped retreating and some are now advancing again. And, frankly, we don't know why."

Global temperature has risen about a degree since the late 19th century; levels of carbon dioxide in the atmosphere have increased by about 30% over the same period and Carbon dioxide should contribute to future warming. These claims are true. Arguments break down, if accepted models are correct, because global warming would reduce the catastrophes which are occurring.

There have been repeated claims that increased hurricane activity is another sign of human-induced climate change. Everything from a heat wave in Paris to heavy snows in Buffalo have been blamed on people burning gasoline to fuel their cars, and coal and natural gas to heat, cool and electrify their homes. Yet how can a barely discernible, one-degree increase in the recorded global mean temperature since the late 19th century possibly gain public acceptance as the source of recent weather catastrophes? And how can it translate into unlikely claims about future catastrophes?

Alarm rather than genuine scientific curiosity, is driving scientific funding and guaranteeing alarming results.

Reforestation and Deforestation

Almost anyone who lives in the rural Northeast can attest that the forest has expanded its range in the past century. That is why all those stone walls — the edges of cleared fields once upon a time — are now orphaned deep in the woods. A new study published by the National Academy of Sciences and based on a recent international assessment of forests confirms that reforestation has become a widespread pattern in well-off countries and also in a few that are not so well off.

This is obviously good news. Forests provide critical wildlife habitat, and the study's authors say the forest "withholds carbon dioxide that would add to greenhouse gas in the atmosphere."

Forest transitions — the shift from net deforestation to reforestation — began long ago in Europe and more recently in the United States. What is surprising is that they are beginning to happen in parts of India and Asia as well. Reforestation is directly linked to prosperity, an indicator that a country has risen well above the level of mere subsistence and has an economy that no longer depends entirely on exploiting natural resources.

In some parts of the world, deforestation is only expanding, with dire consequences for biodiversity and the climate.

And even where forests have recovered, there is the likelihood that they have passed through an ecological point of no return. Some of the most biologically diverse forests are being logged or burned without ceasing, destroying irreplaceable habitat and extinguishing species one by one.

Liberals collide over Redwoods versus Solar Energy

In California, after six years in the courts, a family has been ordered to cut down its redwoods in accordance with the Solar Shade Control Act. Their neighbor installed solar panels in 2001 to take advantage of the California Solar Initiative (short hand for handout) even though the redwoods blocked the sun. Now the redwoods must go and the redwood owners must pay to have them cut down even though they no longer have the money to do so as that went to their lawyers.

Seafood

All seafood stocks around the world may collapse by 2050 if fishing continues at its current rate, scientists have warned, piling intense pressure on industry and governments to handle stocks more sustainably.

The collapse, which would see more than 90 per cent of all wild seafood that is currently fished disappear, would destroy both ecosystems and fishing economies, says a large study, published in the Science journal.

The findings reveal a major threat to fishing sector earnings and put the heaviest pressure yet on both industry and governments to create a more sustainable production chain.

The international team of researchers spent four years trawling through United Nations figures and studies on 48 marine protected areas worldwide, as well as examining coastal regions.

Current declines in biodiversity in the world's oceans were cutting food supplies to a growing human population, sabotaging environments and preventing the sea from filtering out harmful pollutants, they said.

Most European fish stocks are now over fished, according to the influential International Council for the Exploration of the Sea. The increasingly precarious situation was highlighted this year by a World Wildlife Fund study claiming that blue fin tuna stocks had almost been fished out of some of the Mediterranean's oldest fishing grounds.

Many species are capable of bouncing back in between three and 10 years. For now, declining stocks are likely to raise the seafood sector's reliance on farmed produce as governments face up to the fact that the world's oceans are being depleted at unsustainable rates.

Steve Palumbi of Stanford University says "Unless we fundamentally change the way we manage all the oceans' species together, as working ecosystems, then this century is the last century of wild seafood."

Global Warming will get worse as will Traffic Congestion.

Traffic congestion is choking our cities, hurting our economy, and reducing our quality of life," begins a new report from the Reason Foundation, a libertarian think tank. Rush-hour gridlock paralyzes 39,500 lane-miles of roadway each year, eating up $63 billion in lost time and fuel. But much worse is to come.

By 2030, the number of severely congested lane-miles will reach nearly 60,000 per year, an increase of more than 50 percent. Commuters in the largest metropolitan areas will spend 65 percent more time in traffic than they do now. Within 25 years, at least a dozen major cities will be choked with travel delays worse than in today's Los Angeles, whose notorious congestion is the worst in America.

The solution is the obvious one: Build more highways, and manage them more intelligently. 104,000 new lane-miles will be needed by 2030, at a cost of about $21 billion a year, much of which could be raised through electronic tolling. The return on that investment would be a stunning 7.7 billion fewer hours spent in traffic each year, along with all the wealth and freedom those time savings would generate.

We are overwhelmingly a nation of drivers; the real mass transit is the traffic on our highways. If the highways don't grow to keep up with that traffic, the strangulating misery of gridlock will only get worse.

The good news is that the USA will continue to be better than anywhere else.

Gore on Global Warming

Al Gore, the former U.S. vice president who shared the Nobel Peace Prize for helping to alert the world to the danger of global warming has declared that the United States was "principally responsible for obstructing progress" and urged an open-ended deal at a recent meeting in Bali that could be enhanced after Mr. Bush left office in January 2009.

"Over the next two years the United States is going to be somewhere it is not now," Mr. Gore said to loud applause. "You must anticipate that."

Developing nations, notably China and India, have stuck with their longstanding refusal to accept limits on their emissions, despite projections that they will soon become the dominant sources of climate-warming gases.

A system was proposed in Bali that would compensate developing countries for protecting their rain forests, a plan that environmentalists described as an innovative effort to mitigate global warming. Rain forest destruction is a major source of carbon dioxide, and living rain forests, according to recent research, play an important role in absorbing the gas. Precisely how countries with large rain forests, like Indonesia and Brazil, would be compensated has not been worked out.

United Nations officials said part of the financing would come from developed countries through aid and other financing would come from carbon credits traded under the Kyoto pact.

Czech President Vaclav Klaus Says

The basic questions of the current climate change debate are sufficiently known and well structured:

1) Do we live in an era of a statistically significant, non-accidental and non-cyclical climate change?

2) If so, is it dominantly man-made?

3) If so, should such a moderate temperature increase bother us more than many other pressing problems we face and should it receive our extraordinary attention?

4) If we want to change the climate, can it be done? Are current attempts to do so the best allocation of our scarce resources?

My answer to all these questions is NO, but with a difference in emphasis. I don't aspire to measure the global temperature, or to estimate the importance of factors which make it. This is not the area of my comparative advantages. But to argue, as it's done by many contemporary environmentalists, that these questions have already been answered with a consensual "yes" and that there is an unchallenged scientific consensus about this is unjustified. It is also morally and intellectually deceptive.

President Bush would be pilloried if he told the truth in this way instead of having to wrap it up as some protection against Liberal righteousness and hate.

CHAPTER 13
SEPTEMBER 11 AND
ITS AFTERMATH

September 11, 2001

These attacks were consistent with the overall mission statement of al-Qaeda, as set out in a 1998 fatwa issued by Osama bin Laden and Ayman al-Zawahiri. The fatwa lists three main "crimes and sins" committed by the Americans: U.S. military occupation of the Arabian Peninsula, U.S. aggression against the Iraqi people, and U.S. support of Israel. The fatwa also specifically condemns the U.S. for "plundering" the resources of the region, oppressing the people by supporting abusive regimes in the region, and dictating policy to legitimate leaders. It also opposes the presence of U.S. military bases and installations in the region, especially on Muslim holy land, which are used to "threaten" Muslim countries, while fomenting disunity and strife. By a similar token, it decries the continued refusal to address the "occupation of Palestine".

The Persian Gulf War, the ensuing sanctions against Iraq and the bombing of Iraq by the United States were cited in 1998 as further proof of these allegations. The fatwa uses Islamic texts to exhort violent action against American military and citizenry until the alleged grievances are reversed.

Al-Qaeda is an international alliance of militant Sunni jihadist organizations. Its roots can be traced back to Osama bin Laden and others around the time of the Soviet withdrawal from Afghanistan in 1989. Al-Qaeda's objectives include the end of foreign influence in Muslim countries and the creation of a new Islamic caliphate, which is the only form of governance that has full approval in traditional Islamic theology. The caliphate has lain dormant and largely unclaimed since the 1920s, after the collapse of the Ottoman Empire and redistribution of Islamic lands, as a consequence of being on the losing side in World War 1. In recent years though, interest among Muslims in international unity and the Caliphate has grown. Islamic theology and Islamic law are in violent contrast to Christian theology and Western law.

One explanation for the growth of the radical Islamist movement in general and al-Qaeda in particular, was the rivalry between two oil-rich countries - Saudi Arabia and Iran - for leadership of the Muslim world. The version of Islam promoted by the two countries differs in almost every way. The only similarity is that they both promote resurgent Islam.

The Islamic Republic of Iran was revolutionary and republican, where Saudi was traditional and royal. Iran was profoundly anti-American, whereas Saudi was a close anti-Communist ally of the U.S. And Iran was Shia, where Saudi was Wahhabi, which did not even consider Shia to be true Muslims.

The supreme leader of the new Islamic Republic of Iran, Grand Ayatollah Khomeini, promised to export his revolutionary ideology and succeeded in many places including Iraq, countries around the Persian Gulf, and particularly Lebanon where Hezbollah became a major power.

Partly in response, Saudi Arabia generously funded madrasahs (Islamic schools) and other forms of religious education throughout the Muslim world. Saudi Arabia was only one percent of the Muslim world in terms of population, but its billions of dollars in petroleum income supported an estimated 90% of the expenses of the entire Muslim faith.

This vast wealth overrode other more moderate traditions of Islam in favor of Wahhabism, which taught that Muslims should not only "always oppose" infidels "in every way," but "to hate them for their religion ... for Allah's sake," and that Shia and other self-professed Muslims were infidels. Thus extreme and puritanical strictures were spread throughout the Muslim world to young and old from primary madrasahs to high level scholarship.

Another factor contributing to radicalism was economic stagnation of the Arab world and its humiliation and frustration stemming from lack of opportunity except through accepting Western help particularly in establishing the huge economic benefit from its oil reserves.

It is ironic that our dependence on Arab oil is what fuels terrorism against us. Then all it took was a few box cutters and unlocked cockpit doors plus a politically correct refusal to profile likely terrorists or fight back, except on Flight 93, to create chaos in the USA. The aftermath is pretend security at airports where old ladies are dispossessed of their toiletries and everyone is harassed, instead of focusing on the fraction of 1% who are potential terrorists and who still have easy access to airports.

Then there is the loaded question as to why the USA places itself between Iran and Saudi Arabia with the consequence that it is universally hated. Iraq is a pawn in this game of chess.

Waterboarding Works

A former CIA officer who participated in the capture and questioning of the first al-Qaeda terrorist suspect to be waterboarded has said that the harsh technique provided an intelligence breakthrough that "probably saved lives," but that he now regards the tactic as torture.

Zayn Abidin Muhammed Hussein abu Zubaida, the first high-ranking al-Qaeda member captured after the Sept. 11, 2001, attacks, broke in less than a minute after he was subjected to the technique and began providing interrogators with information that led to the disruption of several planned attacks, said John Kiriakou, who served as a CIA interrogator in Pakistan.

Abu Zubaida was one of two detainees whose interrogation was captured in video recordings that the CIA later destroyed. The disclosure of the tapes' destruction ignited a furor on Capitol Hill and allegations that the agency tried to hide evidence of illegal torture.

"It was like flipping a switch," said Kiriakou, the first former CIA employee directly involved in the questioning of "high-value" al-Qaeda detainees to speak publicly.

In an interview, Kiriakou said he did not witness Abu Zubaida's waterboarding but was part of the interrogation team that questioned him in a hospital in Pakistan for weeks after his capture in that country in the spring of 2002.

He described Abu Zubaida as ideologically zealous, defiant and uncooperative — until the day in mid-summer when his captors strapped him to a board, wrapped his nose and mouth in cellophane and forced water into his throat in a technique that simulates drowning.

The waterboarding lasted about 35 seconds before Abu Zubaida broke down, according to Kiriakou, who said he was given a detailed description of the incident by fellow team members. The next day, Abu Zubaida told his captors he would tell them whatever they wanted, Kiriakou said.

"He said that Allah had come to him in his cell and told him to cooperate, because it would make things easier for his brothers," Kiriakou said.

US Liberals Endanger our Protection from Terrorism

A U.N. investigation, encouraged by US Liberals, concluded that the United States committed acts of torture at Guantanamo Bay by force-feeding detainees and subjecting them to prolonged solitary confinement. The report from five person U.N. human rights delegation also recommended that the USA close Guantanamo Bay and cease all special interrogation techniques. It accused the United States of violating the detainees' rights to a fair trial, to freedom of religion and to health. The five person U.N. delegation was appointed to its three-year terms by the 53-nation U.N. Human Rights Commission.

The obvious flaw of the report was that it judged U.S. treatment of detainees according to peacetime human rights laws, ignoring that we are at war on terror. About 500 people were being held in Guantanamo because of links to al-Qaeda. The report dismissed the U.S. claim that the war on terror constitutes an armed conflict.

The delegation had no basis for its statements since it rejected an invitation to visit Guantanamo Bay, because it would not be allowed to interview detainees. Had they visited, they would have found that there is no torture. The United Nations consists of every questionable regime in the world whose main purpose is to embarrass the USA. All that is left now is for our own Liberals to have a field day as they attempt to belittle George Bush (and so the USA) in the eyes of our enemies and of the world.

The same motivations are at work on the issue of warrant less eavesdropping; Attorney General Alberto Gonzales asserted that the resolution authorizing force in Iraq had conferred wiretapping authority on the President. It is clear that it is not possible to disperse information in this area across all branches of government in the guise of checks and balances and then stop terrorists. Nor can the Administration present the paperwork required to satisfy probable cause before a FISA judge prior to antiterrorism wiretaps. The surveillance program could only work to prevent another 9/11 attack if it stayed secret. The odds of it staying secret would diminish as its existence spread through Congress and the Judiciary. Now it is public, its utility is zero. What's left is the legal issue of whether the Bush administration violated the Foreign Intelligence Surveillance Act court (FISA). That will depend on whether we continue to believe that we are at war on terror. What we have lost is a powerful weapon against terrorist attacks and the Bush administration diminished in the eyes of the world. US Liberals have once again made us less secure.

A comparison with UK practices shows how our Liberal obsession with civil rights is overblown. Britain, already the world's leader in video surveillance of its people, will soon be able to monitor the movements of millions of cars so that it can deny criminals, including terrorists, the use of the roads. People in Britain are monitored by more than 4 million closed-circuit cameras, making it the most-watched nation in the world. The benefits of London's network were impressively demonstrated after the subway bombing last July killing fifty-two passengers. Closed-circuit cameras identified the bombers which was a critical element in the subsequent investigation.

Certainly Congress is a forum for competing self-interests and it is competing self-interests that protect our liberties. But propaganda is not self-interest. And though everyone spins information to a certain extent for the sake of persuasion, the Liberals take it a step too far.

They do not discuss the issues themselves; they aggressively attack the intellect, integrity, and intentions of those who are currently making decisions. They attack the United States as if somehow the pursuit of its self-interest is in and of itself evil, and they make the suggestion that perhaps the US and its people deserve the treatment they are getting from the Muslim extremists. It is not a request for accountability; it is nothing short of sabotage.

War against Liberals

There is a yearning for Democratic and Republican lawmakers to reduce their extreme partisanship, look for common ground instead of attacking one another, and start working together to solve some of the problems that affect us all. Years of slash-and-burn politics for selfish or ideological reasons have exhausted the patience of the nation and driven down its faith in government to get things done for the public good.

Do not hold your breath as this rapprochement will not happen any time soon. Indeed we need to pause in our War on Terrorism to confront a more immediate threat to the USA – our own home grown Liberals. They do not have the stomach for world leadership and its inevitable difficulties. Liberals cannot tolerate uncertainty or a competitive environment and are ready to circle the wagons and live in isolation.

Anti-Bush pathology runs so deep among many Liberals that they really do think they are grappling with a potential fascist situation. We have seen the enemy and it is the Liberals in our midst.

If you think Liberals are bad here, Holland is worse. Would-be immigrants to the Netherlands must buy a copy and view a film to test their readiness to participate in the liberal Dutch culture. The camera focuses on two homosexual men kissing in a park. Then a topless woman emerges from the sea and walks on to a crowded beach. Regardless of whether they find the content offensive, applicants must watch this film it if they hope to pass the Netherlands' new entrance examination.

Liberals overblown concerns about civil rights, profiling and privacy and their road blocks to real security screening still leaves us vulnerable to be blown out of the skies.

In the most recent Government test, federal investigators were able to carry materials needed to make a homemade bomb through security screening at 21 US airports. In every case, no machine, no swab, no screener anywhere stopped the bomb materials from getting through. Even when investigators deliberately triggered extra screening of bags, no one discovered the materials.

Partisan politics prevent any real progress in homeland security.

CHAPTER 14
WAR ON TERRORISM

What Osama Wants

A total withdrawal from Iraq would play into the hands of the jihadist terrorists. As Osama bin Laden's deputy, Ayman al-Zawahri, made clear shortly after 9/11 in his book "Knights Under the Prophet's Banner," Al Qaeda's most important short-term strategic goal is to seize control of a state, or part of a state, somewhere in the Muslim world. "Confronting the enemies of Islam and launching jihad against them require a Muslim authority, established on a Muslim land," he wrote. "Without achieving this goal our actions will mean nothing." Such a jihadist state would be the ideal launching pad for future attacks on the West.

US Liberal pussyfooting fits all too neatly into Osama bin Laden's master narrative about American foreign policy. His theme is that America is a paper tiger that cannot tolerate body bags coming home; to back it up, he cites Vietnam and, more recently, President Clinton's decision in the early 1990s to pull troops from Somalia. A unilateral pullout from Iraq would only confirm this analysis of American weakness among his jihadist allies.

Indeed, in 2005 Zawahri sent Zarqawi a letter, which was intercepted by the United States military, exhorting him to start preparing for the impending American withdrawal similar to that of Vietnam 30 years ago. For the United States to wash its hands of the country now would give Al Qaeda's leaders what they want.

The US should abandon its Liberal pretensions that it can make Iraq a functioning democracy and halt the civil war. Instead, we should focus on a minimalist definition of our interests in Iraq, which is to prevent a militant jihadist mini-state from emerging and allowing Al Qaeda to regroup.

A significant US force must remain in Iraq for many years to destroy Al Qaeda in the Middle East. That can be accomplished by making the American presence less visible; withdrawing American troops to bases in central and western Iraq; and relying on contingents of Special Forces to hunt militants just as we did when we captured the 'Osama bin Laden of the Sahara' in Chad in 2004.

Insurgencies are not defeated by conventional ground forces any more than are other brands of terrorism.

Al Qaeda Victorious

The jihadists understand that they are fighting a war of ideas. According to "The Management of Savagery," Al Qaeda manual, the success of the movement will ultimately depend on the jihadists' ability to damage America's prestige throughout the globe, sow discord between America and its allies and expose the hollowness of American values.

Standing up to Terrorists

If you were one of the journalists kidnapped in Gaza and ordered at gunpoint to become a Muslim, what would you have done? Fox News reporter Steve Centanni and photographer Olaf Wiig announced their acceptance of Islam on a videotape released by their kidnappers -- ``because they had the guns," Centanni later said, ``and we didn't know what the hell was going on."

Whether their acquiescence was an act of cowardice or of prudence, reasonable people can debate. Clearly it wasn't their only choice.

Fabrizio Quattrocchi, an Italian security guard taken hostage in Iraq in 2004. Quattrocchi's jihadi captors, intending to make a video of an infidel's craven death, ordered him to kneel beside an open grave with a hood on his head. Defiantly, he stood up, tried to rip off the hood, and shouted, ``I will show you how an Italian dies!" They murdered him an instant later, but he died bravely, on his feet, refusing with his last breath to be humiliated by savages.

Less Political Correctness

The reason we have not been attacked on American soil is that the war started by radical Muslims is not against the United States, but against everyone who does not conform to their beliefs and way of life. It is the first global war we have experienced since globalization became a factor in our life, and the terrorist battlefield has included Madrid, London, Bali, Moscow, Egypt, Iraq, Jordan, Saudi Arabia and India. The terrorists have had a very busy five years.

The struggle imposed on us is, by nature, a long-term struggle. Only an effective homeland security system will provide us with the necessary political power to prevail in those instances where the terrorists do find value in attacking within the United States. In that sense, we must be less politically correct, and begin a program that looks for risks where they are most likely to be found. For example, it is crucial to identify high-risk airline passengers through all criteria — including appearance and behavior — and spend more resources on them, rather than maintaining an across-the-board, politically correct low level of search.

Jihad Progress

Australia: Australia's foremost Muslim cleric triggers an uproar when he likens women who don't wear an Islamic headscarf to "uncovered meat" and blames them for attracting sexual predators. "If you take out uncovered meat and place it outside on the street, or in the garden or the park . . . and the cats come and eat it," says Sheik Taj al-Din Hilali, "whose fault is it, the cats' or the uncovered meat? If [the woman] was in her room, in her home, in her headscarf, no problem would have occurred."

Afghanistan: The kidnappers of Italian photojournalist Gabriele Torsello threaten to murder him unless Abdul Rahman, an Afghan Christian convert, is returned to Afghanistan and handed over to an Islamic court. Rahman lives in Italy, which granted him asylum earlier this year, when he faced the death penalty under Afghanistan's sharia law for converting from Islam to Christianity.

Iran: The president of Iran calls Israel "a group of terrorists" and threatens to harm any country that supports the Jewish state. "This is an ultimatum," warns Mahmoud Ahmadinejad, who has called for the elimination of Israel and the United States. "Don't complain tomorrow." Days later, the deputy director of Iran's Atomic Energy Organization confirms another stride forward for the country's illicit nuclear program: With the injection of gas into a second cascade of centrifuges, Iran has doubled its uranium-enrichment capacity.

Thailand: Islamist terrorists bomb a column of Buddhist monks as they collect offerings of food in Narathiwat, a city in southern Thailand. One person is killed; 12 are injured. The attack is the latest in a bloody week that has included multiple shootings and another fatal bombing.

France: Another Muslim intifadah rages in France. Hundreds of cars are torched nightly and passenger buses set ablaze with Molotov cocktails. One such fire in Marseille leaves a 26-year-old woman in a coma with burns covering 70 percent of her body. "We are in a state of civil war, orchestrated by radical Islamists," says police union leader Michel Thoomis. "This is not a question of urban violence any more. It is an intifadah, with stones and firebombs." So far this year, more than 2,500 police have been wounded in clashes with rioters.

Britain: In a "true Islamic state," sexually active homosexuals would be executed, says Arshad Misbahi, an imam in Manchester's Central Mosque. According to interviewer John Casson, the imam explains that while executions "might result in the deaths of thousands," they would be worthwhile "if this deterred millions from having sex and spreading disease."

NATO forces have recently killed scores of Taliban fighters in Afghanistan, trying to kill them. Czech intelligence agents thwarted an Islamist plan to seize the Central Synagogue in Prague on Rosh Hashanah, hold the Jewish worshipers hostage, and then blow up the building with its occupants. A proposal to let Muslim taxi drivers at the Minneapolis-St. Paul International Airport refuse service to passengers carrying alcohol was scrapped in the wake of vehement public opposition. And the world's mightiest fighting force continues to kill Islamofascists in Iraq, currently the key battleground in the global jihad.

There can't be much question that at this point in the war against radical Islam, the radicals are on the march. From Ahmadinejad's swagger to Hezbollah's war on Israel to the plot to blow up jetliners leaving London, our enemies are aggressive, relentless, and unequivocal in their determination to defeat us. Meanwhile, Western Europe is turning into Eurabia before our eyes, as a fading native population with its effete secular culture of pacifism and relativism is superseded by a surging Muslim cohort. Most Muslims are not Islamists or terrorists, of course. However, most of them keep quiet in the face of the radical offensive. That is all the radicals need to keep driving the jihad forward.

"If this country lets down its guard, it will be a fatal mistake," President Bush said last week. Yet too many Americans seem unable to recognize the threat, or to believe that they, their liberties, and the lives of innumerable human beings are truly at stake in a deadly global war.

Radical Islam is not going away. Like Nazism and communism, it is (in Senator Rick Santorum's words) "an ideology that produces the systemic murder of innocents." Like those earlier totalitarianisms, it will go on murdering until it is crushed. Like them, it is impervious to appeasement and contemptuous of weakness. The longer Americans sleep, the farther the jihad advances.

Taliban

Abdul Baqi, an Afghan Taliban fighter in his 20's fresh from the front in Helmand Province in southern Afghanistan, had just lost five friends fighting British troops and had seen many others killed or wounded by bombs as they sheltered inside a mosque.

He was now looking forward to taking a logic course at a madrasa, or religious school, near Peshawar during his holiday. Pakistan's religious parties, he told me through an interpreter, would lodge him, as they did other Afghan Taliban fighters, and keep him safe. With Abdul Baqi was his mentor, Mullah Sadiq, who was auditing Taliban finances and arranging logistics. He had just dispatched nine fighters to Afghanistan and had taken wounded men to a hospital in Islamabad.

Although Mullah Sadiq said they had lost many commanders in battles around Kandahar, he and Abdul Baqi appeared to be in good spirits, laughing and chatting loudly on a cell phone to Taliban friends in Pakistan and Afghanistan. After all, they never imagined that the Taliban would be back so soon or in such force or that they would be giving such trouble to the Afghan government of Hamid Karzai and some 40,000 NATO and U.S. troops in the country. For the first time since the fall of 2001, when the Taliban were overthrown, they were beginning to taste the possibility of victory.

Since 2002, the American and Pakistani militaries have focused on North Waziristan and South Waziristan, two of the seven districts making up Pakistan's semiautonomous tribal areas, which are between the North-West Frontier Province and, to the south, Baluchistan Province; in the days since the 9/11 attacks, some tribes there had sheltered members of Al Qaeda and spawned their own Taliban movement. Meanwhile, in the deserts of Baluchistan, whose capital, Quetta, is just a few hours' drive from the Afghan city of Kandahar, the Afghan Taliban were openly reassembling themselves under Mullah Omar and his leadership council. Quetta has become a kind of free zone where strategies could be formed, funds picked up, interviews given and victories relished.

How is it that the Taliban is making a comeback five years after American and Afghan forces drove them from power? What kind of experience would lead Afghans to reject what seemed to be an emerging democratic government? Had we missed something that made Taliban rule appealing? Were they the only opposition the aggrieved could turn to? Or, as many Afghans are saying, was Pakistan up to its old tricks — cooperating with the Americans and Karzai while conspiring to bring back the Taliban, who had been valued "assets" before 9/11?

In Kabul, Kandahar and Pakistan, pro-Taliban video discs and tapes are in the markets. They invoke nostalgia for the jihad against the Russians and inspire their viewers to rise up again. One begins with clattering Chinooks disgorging American soldiers into the desert. Then we see the new Afghan government onstage, focusing in on the Northern Alliance warlords — Abdul Rashid Dostum, Burhanuddin Rabbani, Karim Khalili, Muhammad Fahim, Ismail Khan, Abdul Sayyaf. It cuts to American soldiers doing push-ups and pinpointing targets on maps; next it shows bombs the size of bathtubs dropping from planes and missiles emblazoned with "Royal Navy" rocketing through the sky; then it moves to hospital beds and wounded children. Message: America and Britain brought back the warlords and bombed your children. In the next clip, there are metal cages under floodlights and men in orange jumpsuits, bowed and crouching. It cuts back to the wild eyes of John Walker Lindh and shows trucks hauling containers crammed with young Afghan and Pakistani prisoners — Taliban, hundreds of whom would suffocate to death in those containers, supposedly at the command of the warlord and current army chief of staff, General Dostum. Then back to American guards wheeling hunger-striking Guantánamo prisoners on gurneys. Interspliced are older images, a bit fuzzy, of young Afghan men, hands tied behind their backs, heads bowed, hauled off by Communist guards. The message: Foreigners have invaded our lands again; Americans, Russians — no difference.

During the period from 1994 to 2001, the Taliban were a cloistered clique with little interest in global affairs. Today they are far more sophisticated and outward-looking. "The Taliban of the 90's were concerned with their district or province," says Waheed Muzhda, a senior aide at the Supreme Court in Kabul, who before the Taliban fell worked in their Foreign Ministry. "Now they have links with other networks. Before, only two Internet connections existed — one was with Mullah Omar's office and the other at the Foreign Ministry here in Kabul. Now they are connected to the world." Though this is still very much an Afghan insurgency, fueled by complex local grievances and power struggles, the films sold in the markets of Pakistan and Afghanistan merge the Taliban story with that of the larger struggle of the Muslim umma, the global community of Islam: images of U.S. soldiers in Iraq and Israelis dragging off young Palestinian men and throwing off Palestinian mothers clinging to their sons. In the Taliban story, Special Forces soldiers desecrate the bodies of Taliban fighters by burning them, the Koran is desecrated in Guantánamo toilets, the Prophet Muhammad is desecrated in Danish cartoons and finally an apostate, Abdul Rahman, the Afghan who was arrested earlier this year for converting to Christianity, desecrates Islam and is not only not punished but is released and flown off to Italy.

It is not at all clear that Afghans want the return of a Taliban government. But even sophisticated Kabulis told me that they are fed up with corruption. And in the Pashtun regions, which make up about half the country, Afghans are fed up with five years of having their homes searched and the young men of their villages rounded up in the name of counterinsurgency. Earlier this month in Kabul, Gen. David Richards, the British commander of NATO's Afghanistan force, imagined what Afghans are thinking: "They will say, 'We do not want the Taliban, but then we would rather have that austere and unpleasant life than another five years of fighting.'" He estimated that if NATO didn't succeed in bringing substantial economic development to Afghanistan soon, some 70 percent of Afghans would shift their loyalty to the Taliban.

The President's Plan

As a result of Sept. 11, 2001, President Bush has transformed the way we fight terrorism and the tools we use. We successfully attack those very things our enemies need to operate and survive: leadership, communications, the ability to travel, weapons; foot soldiers and financing. The President has strengthened and transformed the intelligence community, integrated our military and intelligence assets, and broken down the barriers that kept domestic law enforcement and intelligence agencies from sharing information.

The United States has enhanced relationships with allies around the world, recognizing that this is truly a global war on terrorism. Working together, we have denied Al Qaeda the safe havens and resources it needs to plan and carry out attacks and made it more difficult for our enemies to travel. We use their communications against them and have cut off their money.

At home, the President has transformed the fight by creating the Department of Homeland Security and by ensuring that the F.B.I. had the necessary tools, like the Patriot Act, to get the job done. The airline bombing plot disrupted by Britain this summer is only the most recent case of brutal terrorists continuing to plan mass murder. We are in a war we did not ask for, but it is a war we must wage and a war we will win, so long as we defeat our own Liberals first.

CHAPTER 15
M-WORD

Avoiding the M-word

Notable British voices spoke out in defense of Islam after Britain's most recent terrorist near-misses -- the two unexploded car bombs in London's West End and the fiery SUV rammed into the main terminal at Glasgow's international airport.

Britain's prime minister, Gordon Brown declared that the word "Muslim" must not be used in connection with terrorism, and insisted that even the phrase "war on terror" should be scrapped.

London Mayor Ken Livingstone cautioned against pointing a finger at Islam, contending that in London, "Muslims are less likely to support the use of violence to achieve political ends than non-Muslims."

Daud Abdullah, deputy secretary general of the Muslim Council of Britain when asked whether Muslim extremists might be responsible for the attempted atrocities in London and Glasgow, counseled: "Let's avoid presumptions. It can be the work of Muslims, Christians, Jews, or Buddhists."

By contrast, Hassan Butt, a onetime spokesman for the radical Islamist organization al-Muhajiroun, who has renounced his former life, noted the resemblance of the latest terror attempts to other recent British Islamic extremist plots and pinpointed Islamic theology as the real engine of our violence. He described British jihadists as mindless killers who had declared war on the rest of the world.

Just days before the second anniversary of the deadly 7/7 London transit bombings, and less than a year since 24 British Muslims were arrested for plotting to blow up passenger jets over the Atlantic, Brown, Livingstone and Abdullah, in their attempt to be politically correct, spoke as if they had no inkling that Britain is a battleground in militant Islam's global jihad.

Butt emphasized that jihadists are motivated not by opposition to British or US foreign policy but by a fundamentalist theology that seeks to subject the entire world to "Islamic justice." Radical Imams teach their followers that they must fight for Dar al-Islam (the House of Islam) against Dar al-Harb (the House of War -- i.e., infidels to be defeated). And "in Dar el-Harb, anything goes, including the treachery and cowardice of attacking civilians."

By turning a blind eye to the radical theology of the jihadists, Butt says, mainstream Muslim institutions and political leaders like Brown and Livingstone make it easy for the extremists to recruit new followers. They refuse to broach the difficult and often complex truth that Islam can be interpreted as condoning violence against the unbeliever -- and instead repeat the mantra that Islam is peace, and hope that by their words the violence will go away.

Wars cannot be won through denial and willful blindness. Yet, Liberal Western leaders and institutions deliberately avert their gaze from the reality of the Islamist threat. UN Secretary General Ban Ki-Moon blames global warming, not Sudan's jihadist regime, for the genocide being carried out in Darfur. The Liberal Presidential candidates for President, Senators Barack Obama and Hilary Clinton are in a convenient mind set of denial. They maintain lavish campaign websites, complete with detailed position papers that have nothing to say about radical Islam's aggressive war.

The New York Times, reporting the Glasgow attack on Page 1, carefully avoided using the M-word to identify Britain's Muslim terrorists. Instead it attributed the 7/7 bombings to Britain's "disenfranchised South Asian population" and reported that the terrorists in Glasgow "were South Asian." (Indian Hindus are the United Kingdom's largest South Asian demographic.) Similarly, seven reporters contributed to AP's story on the arrested jihad-doctors ("Diverse group allegedly in British plot"), yet somehow missed the radical theology they shared.

Liberal political correctness is no strategy for victory. Islamic fascists will not hate us less if we avoid all mention of the theology that inflames them. Winning the war the jihadists have declared -- the war of Dar al-Islam and Dar al-Harb -- begins with our own moral clarity. The real danger is that Liberals seem to be incapable of understanding anything other than their own pious self-righteousness.

The Problem in Britain

Britain's intelligence chief has said that the country's spy agency is watching dozens of

groups and has foiled several terror-related plots since the July 2005 attacks in London.

Eliza Manningham-Buller, who has headed Britain's domestic intelligence agency, MI5, since 2002, said in a speech that officials were "aware of numerous plots to kill people and to damage our economy," the British Broadcasting Corp. reported on its Web site.

"What do I mean by numerous? Five? Ten?" she said in a rare appearance before a small audience of academics. "Nearer 30 that we currently know."

"These plots often have linked back to al-Qaeda in Pakistan, and through those links al-Qaeda gives guidance and training to its largely British foot soldiers here on an extensive and growing scale," she said.

In early July 2005, four suicide bombers killed 52 people on three subway trains and a bus. Two weeks later, similar attacks were attempted but failed. Three of the four perpetrators of the earlier attacks were British-born.

Manningham-Buller said some of the plots the MI5 is investigating could be less threatening than the deadly 2005 ones, but that they still must be investigated.

MI5 agents are currently watching 200 groups or networks, "actively engaged in plotting, or facilitating, terrorist acts here and overseas," she said, acknowledging it was likely there were more people involved in plots that the security services were not aware of.

Manningham-Buller warned that radicalization, especially of young people, was one of the biggest problems facing anti-terror investigators.

"It is the youth who are being actively targeted, groomed, radicalized and set on a path that frighteningly quickly could end in their involvement in mass murder of their fellow UK citizens," she said. "Young teenagers are being groomed to be suicide bombers."

Interference in Pakistan

In recent years, Pakistan has been the home of banks that wired money for the 9/11 plot, been the chief source of illicit nuclear proliferation, offered a tribal-area haven for planners of worldwide terrorism, abetted the reconstitution of the Taliban and educated many a suicide bomber in Islamic religious schools.

At the same time, President Pervez Musharraf, in power since a 1999 coup, has received about $10 billion in U.S. aid, much of it to reinforce the Pakistani military in fighting Al Qaeda, the Taliban and global jihadism in South Waziristan and other tribal areas.

The assassination of Benazir Bhutto, the corrupt recycled Oxford-educated former prime minister who returned from exile on Oct. 18 under a flawed US and British mediated plan to shift Pakistan to democratic rule is a further botched American attempt to manage a nuclear-armed Islamic state.

It's not clear who killed Bhutto, although hers was a chronicle of a death foretold. Musharraf's government, says that Baitullah Mehsud, a militant with links to Al Qaeda and the Taliban, was behind it. Al Qaeda has turned more of its attention from Afghanistan to the richer rewards of upending Pakistan.

Four years of strong Capitalistic economic growth have expanded a Pakistani middle class that wants democracy's rule of law. Radical Islamist parties constitute a minority: unlike Iran, democratic forces outweigh the theocratic.

If Afghanistan is ready for democracy, Pakistan certainly is, but it could be that neither is ready. Either way, the USA should stop its Liberal do-gooding around the world in the mistaken belief that everywhere should become a mini-version of the USA. If we truly believe in diversity, we should leave other political institutions alone, whether they are tribal, feudal, Islamic or Communist. We should allow Capitalism to work in its own time.

Muslim Immigration into USA

As the United States wrestles with questions of terrorism, civil liberties and immigration control, Muslims appear to be moving here again in surprising numbers, according to statistics collected by the Department of Homeland Security and the Census Bureau.

Immigrants from predominantly Muslim countries in the Middle East, North Africa and Asia are planting new roots in states from Virginia to Texas to California.

In 2005, more people from Muslim countries became legal permanent United States residents — nearly 96,000 — than in any year in the previous two decades.

More than 40,000 of them were admitted last year, the highest annual number since the terrorist attacks, according to data on 22 countries provided by the Department of Homeland Security.

Many have made the journey unbowed by tales of immigrant hardship, and despite their own opposition to American policy in the Middle East. They come seeking the same promise that has drawn foreigners to the United States for many decades, according to a range of experts and immigrants: economic opportunity and political freedom. Those lures, both powerful and familiar, have been enough to conquer fears that America is an inhospitable place for Muslims.

Muslims have been settling in the United States in significant numbers since the mid-1960s, after immigration quotas that favored Eastern Europeans were lifted. Spacious mosques opened in Chicago, Los Angeles and New York as a new, highly educated Muslim population took hold. Over the next three decades, Muslim migration to the United States was marked by growth and prosperity. A larger percentage of immigrants from Muslim countries have graduate degrees than other American residents, and their average salary is about 20 percent higher, according to census data. Up to six million Muslims live in the United States.

The Increasing Influence of Islam

In the Middle East disillusionment and hostility toward national governments move many young people to adopt Islam as an identity, supplanting nationality or ethnicity. It also underscores a challenge facing many Arab countries where local customs and heritage are being abandoned by young people who instead adopt the dress, customs and behavior of conservative Islam. Anger is felt by young people with no work, who now see the world via satellite television and the Internet.

Religious extremism began to be a problem in the 1980's, just as the tribal traditions that governed the people of the Sinai for centuries were slowly being undermined both by the state and by a rising influence of Islamic religious ideology. The Muslim Brotherhood from Egypt and Wahhabism in Saudi Arabia have been particularly virulent.

Afghanistan Heroin

Afghanistan's opium harvest has reached the highest levels ever recorded,

The increase in cultivation has been significantly fueled by the resurgence of Taliban rebels in the south, the country's prime opium growing region. As the insurgents have stepped up attacks, they have also encouraged and profited from the drug trade, promising protection to growers if they expanded their opium operations. The annual harvest is 6,100 metric tons of opium, which is 92 percent of total world supply, exceeding global consumption by 30 percent. The previous record was 4,600 metric tons, set in 1999 while the Taliban governed the country. The area cultivated has increased by 59 percent, with more than 400,000 acres planted with poppies in 2006 compared with less than 260,000 in 2005.

President Hamid Karzai has urged the international community to expand its commitment to strengthen the Afghan police and law enforcement agencies. The Bush administration has made poppy eradication a major facet of its aid to Afghanistan, and it has criticized Mr. Karzai for not doing more to challenge warlords involved in opium production.

The increase in cultivation is mainly a result of the strength of the insurgency in southern Afghanistan, which has left whole districts outside of government control, and the continuing impunity of everyone involved, from the farmers and traffickers to corrupt police and government officials,

35 percent of Afghanistan's gross domestic product comes from the narcotics trade.

CHAPTER 16
IRAQ

An Audiotape from Al-Zawahri's Cave

Al-Qaeda's No. 2 leader has claimed that five years of U.S. involvement in Iraq brought only defeat, and said President Bush will be forced to pass the problem to his successor.

Ayman al-Zawahri alleged that by heeding advice of his top commanders in Iraq and guaranteeing a heavy American military presence after July, Bush was "covering up for the failure" of his Iraq policies.

"If the American forces leave, they will lose everything. And if they stay, they will bleed to death," he argued.

He called for Muslim support of jihad in Iraq, and for backing al-Qaeda's affiliate there, the so-called Islamic State of Iraq.

Al-Zawahri also blasted Sunni fighters who switched sides and joined the American push to pacify Sunni areas of Iraq, the so-called "Awakening Councils."

"Weren't these Awakening (Councils) supposed to hasten the departure of the American forces, or are these Awakenings in need of someone to defend them and protect them," al-Zawahri asked.

He also reiterated a recent statement allegedly by Osama bin Laden that from Iraq the mujahideen will launch a fight to "liberate" Jerusalem.

"Iraq nowadays is the most important battlefield on which our mujahedeen are waging a war against the forces of the Zionist-Christian

Crusade," al-Zawahri said. "Therefore, supporting the mujahedeen in Iraq and especially the Islamic State of Iraq is a most important duty."

Al-Zawahri also slammed anti-American Shiite cleric Muqtada al-Sadr, who has ordered his militia to halt attacks on American and Iraqi forces. He "has become the laughing stock of the world" and is a "toy" in Iran's hands, he said.

Al-Zawahri also criticized the "exploitation of Muslims" in Egypt, his homeland, as well as the plight of Palestinians in the Israel-besieged Gaza.

Al-Zawahri and our own Liberals are in agreement about US failures. Al-Qaeda knows how to exploit out own week kneed Liberal opinions and positions to our detriment.

Deaths in Iraq

The core conflict is one pitting Sunni Muslims against Shiites. Illegal militias have become entrenched, especially in Baghdad neighborhoods where they are seen as providers of security as well as basic social services.

Sectarian violence is fed by neighboring Iran and Syria and driven by a vocal minority of religious extremists who oppose the idea of a democratic Iraq.

Death squads targeting mainly Iraqi civilians will remain a constant problem, heightening the risk of civil war.

Sectarian fighting between minority Sunnis, who controlled Iraq under Saddam Hussein, and the majority Shiites, who are ascending in power after decades of oppression, defines the continuing nature of violence in Iraq.

The security situation is currently at its most complex since the initiation of Operation Iraq Freedom," A Pentagon report said, using the U.S. military's name for the war that was launched in March 2003 to topple Saddam Hussein. This complexity will continue as al-Qaeda, Iran, Syria, Saudi Arabia, Palestine and the various terrorist groups they support, derive benefit, as they perceive it, from the ensuing chaos. The defining difference between US public opinion and them, is that US Liberals count any death toll as morally unacceptable (particularly US lives) whereas they count it as victory, regardless of whose lives are lost so long as, individually, it is not their own.

The View from Iraq

Iraqi President Jalal Talabani has predicted that fighting in Iraq will have abated by the end of 2007, and that Iraqi forces will be able to handle any remaining violence. The U.S. military said the arrest of al-Qaeda in Iraq's second in command, Hamed Jumaa Farid al-Saeedi, which took place in June, 2006, was the most significant blow to the terror network since the death of al-Qaeda in Iraq leader Abu Musab al-Zarqawi.

The truth is that the violence will ebb and flow until attitudes change diametrically in the Middle East. We should not hold our collective breaths for that to happen in any acceptable timeframe. Instead the US Congress and Liberal media should adjust their expectations. US forces should establish a permanent base in Iraq, but should not continue to police Iraq. They should train the Iraqis to do so and should leave it to them. The ensuing violence is their concern and not ours. It is better that our military is based in the trouble spots around the world and not in the USA. Why else do we have a standing military? It should cost little more for them to be based in Iraq than in the USA. The cost of our military adventure in Iraq, now being measured in the trillions of dollars, is unacceptable. We need a well trained task force capability that can cope with guerilla warfare at low cost, not ever more sophisticated weaponry. Let us learn from Britain's success in Malaysia against communist insurgents. It took twelve years but at low cost.

Civil War

The male of the species seems to have the need to resolves issues and claim dominance through combat. Presumably the Sunnis and Shiites will only come to a peaceful resolution after they have shed a great deal more blood. All that we must do is to make sure that we do not become the enemy of both factions by trying to get between them. Harold

Wilson made that mistake when he sent British troops into Northern Ireland. As the revisionists rewrite history, these British troops are now blamed for the terrorism of the IRA.

The same is already happening in the Middle East with much more serious consequences as the Sunnis and Shiites position themselves for civil war. Our own Liberal revisionists have already emasculated us as a military power while we are still in the middle between the protagonists. They blame the US Administration (together with an 'acquiescent' British Government) and the Israelis, as they fawn to seek favor with terrorist regimes in Iran and Syria (governments that support terrorism are in themselves terrorist regimes). The spectacle in the media of British sailors and marines seized by Iran in Iraqi waters, shows how pathetic the once greatest navy in the world has become. Liberals have insisted that we send mothers, with babies at home, to the front line without enough training to know how to behave if captured.

Iraq End Game

It was inevitable that the Arabs would regard the liberation of Iraq through the prism of their own experience. We upended an order of power in Baghdad, dominated as it had been by the minority Sunni Arabs under a brutal dictator; and we emancipated the Shiite stepchildren of the Arab world, as well as the Kurds. Our innocence was astounding. We set the Shia on the present course. We did for them what they could not have done on their own. Our Liberals then recast this liberation into invasion and occupation so condemning the West into being the aggressors and making the Islamists into the victims. We do not need any enemies when we have our own Liberals as friends.

Our only course now is to establish a secure base in Iraq for strategic reasons.

Rumsfeld and Cheney on Iraq

Comparing terrorist groups to a "new type of fascism," Mr. Rumsfeld said, "With the growing lethality and the increasing availability of weapons, can we truly afford to believe that somehow, some way, vicious extremists can be appeased?"

Mr. Cheney has consistently said, "This is not an enemy that can be ignored, or negotiated with, or appeased. Every retreat by civilized nations is an invitation to further violence against us. Men who despise freedom will attack freedom in any part of the world, and so responsible nations have a duty to stay on the offensive, together, to remove this threat."

Mr. Rumsfeld has warned explicitly against appeasement comparing it to the error of appeasing Hitler.

"This enemy is serious, lethal and relentless," he said in his last speech before leaving office as Secretary of State. "But this is not well recognized or fully understood."

President Bush on Iraq

If we pull our military out, we would be handing Iraq over to our worst enemies -Saddam's former henchmen, armed groups with ties to Iran, and al-Qaida terrorists from all over the world who would suddenly have a base of operations far more valuable than Afghanistan under the Taliban.

"The war we fight today is more than a military conflict," Bush said, "It is the decisive ideological struggle of the 21st century."

Bush described the violence in the Middle East and the recently thwarted attack to blow up planes over the Atlantic Ocean as part of the same movement that resulted in the Sept. 11 attacks.

Bush said. "They are successors to fascists, to Nazis, to communists and other totalitarians of the 20th century. And history shows what the outcome will be.

"This war will be difficult. This war will be long. And this war will end in the defeat of the terrorists," Bush said.

"Despite their differences, these groups form the outline of a single movement, a worldwide network of radicals that use terror to kill those who stand in the way of their totalitarian ideology," he said. "And the unifying feature of this movement, the link that spans sectarian divisions and local grievances, is the rigid conviction that free societies are a threat to their twisted view of Islam."

CHAPTER 17
IRAN

US Options for Iran

By undermining US foreign policy, US Liberals have removed any options that we have for preventing Iran from developing a nuclear weapons capability. All of our efforts should now be directed at assessing when they will have this capability and what dominoes will fall as a result. For starters both Saudi Arabia and Turkey will also develop a nuclear bomb. The United Nations will continue to tie US hands through meaningless resolutions that no one will enforce. Iran knows that we are powerless. We should stop appearing to be naïve by pretending that we are not. The unintended consequence of the ongoing conflict in Iraq is that Liberals now rule in the USA even if they do not have control of Congress.

For their part, the Iranians will press on. The spectacle of power they display is illusory. It is a broken society over which the mullahs rule. A society that throws on the scene a leader of Mahmoud Ahmadinejad's derangement is not an orderly land; foreigners may not be able to overthrow that regime, but countries can atrophy as their leaders armed, here, by an oil windfall of uncertain duration strut on the world stage. Iran's is a deeper culture than Iraq's, possessed of a keen sense of Persia's primacy in the region around it. What Iranians make of their own history will not wait on the kind of society that will emerge in Iraq. On the margins, a scholarly tradition given to moderation could be a boon to the clerics of Iran.

In the end the Iranians might eventually become an unlikely ally since Iran will not know deliverance from the sterility of their world if Iraq were to fail. Their joy over an American debacle in Iraq will have to be brief. A raging fire next door to them would be a disaster. And, crafty players, the Iranians know what Liberals in America do not: that Iraq is an unwieldy land, that the Arab-Persian divide in culture, language and temperament will not be bridged.

The thought that US Liberal appeasers will shortly be calling the shots in US foreign policy is an alarming prospect

Iran Superpower

Iran wishes to lead a Muslim bloc that could rival the United States, Europe, and China for global influence. Iran has edged closer to the brink of international confrontation by rejecting demands from the UN Security Council that it suspend uranium enrichment, a key step in developing nuclear weapons, as a precondition for further negotiations. Iran says the program aims to generate electricity for peaceful purposes but the United Nations, Europe, and the United States know that it is a covert weapons program.

Bowing to Iran

Even though Iran blew off the UN Security Council's deadline to stop enriching uranium, the US State Department was still prepared to issue a visa authorizing one of Iran's leading theocrats, former president Mohammad Khatami, to embark on a propaganda tour of the United States. Their explanation for the decision allowing Khatami to enter the United States was that:

``We recognize that former President Khatami headed a regime that is a leading sponsor of terrorism (and) human rights abuses, and presided over Iran's secret nuclear program which is now the focus of possible UN action. After careful deliberation, however, we determined that issuing Mr. Khatami a limited visa, and allowing Mr. Khatami to present his views directly to the American people, will demonstrate to Iran that the United States upholds its commitment to freedom and democracy."

The former president of the world's oldest and most dangerous Islamist dictatorship conducted a multi-city US speaking tour, with appearances in Chicago, New York, the National Cathedral in Washington and an address at Harvard University, Boston on the 'Ethics of Tolerance in the Age of Violence'. Talk now is cheap. Hundreds of dissident students were arrested and tortured during his tenure as president.

His style is to use less incendiary rhetoric than his successor, Mahmoud Ahmadinejad, but he is just as committed to Khomeini's radical revolution and its goal of worldwide Islamist rule. In his own writings, Khatami has insisted that 'only those who have attended religious seminaries should have a voice in government'. As minister of culture and Islamic guidance in the 1980s, he oversaw the creation of Hezbollah. During the recent war in Lebanon, he hailed Hezbollah as ``a shining sun that illuminates and warms the hearts of all Muslims." Throughout Khatami's term of office, the US State Department identified Iran as the world's foremost state sponsor of terrorism.

Iran's Holocaust International Cartoon Contest

The propaganda exhibition by Iran's President Mahmoud Ahmadinejad in Tehran included a caricature of an orthodox Jew with an egregiously long nose that impales an Arab figure; the nose is labeled ``Holocaust." Another depicts the Statue of Liberty holding a book on the Holocaust in one hand and raising the other hand in a Nazi salute.

In a revealing interview with the German weekly Der Spiegel, Ahmadinejad acted as though the reality of the Holocaust is unproven. He cited European laws against Holocaust denial as proof that the West fears a free debate about the historical truth of the Holocaust. He went on to suggest that "if the Holocaust occurred, then Europe must draw the consequences," implying that Europe should provide a state for the Jews. And then he added: "If it did not occur, then the Jews have to go back to where they came from. I believe that the German people today are also prisoners of the Holocaust." In other words, Germans would side with Ahmadinejad if only they had not been made to feel guilty by the myth of the Holocaust.

Ahmadinejad's wish to destroy Israel is most alarming. Even more alarming is the United Nations' indifference to his threats. Why does the world not denounce his hatred of Jews? Is the world now indifferent to the lesson of Nazi Germany?

CHAPTER 18
LOOKING BACK

Donald Rumsfeld

"Today, it should be clear that not only is weakness provocative," Mr. Rumsfeld said when he resigned as Secretary of State, standing at with President Bush and Vice President Dick Cheney at his side, "but the perception of weakness on our part can be provocative as well."

It was a clear parting shot at those considering a withdrawal from war that would define his legacy and that of the President.

"A conclusion by our enemies that the United States lacks the will or the resolve to carry out missions that demand sacrifice and demand patience is every bit as dangerous as an imbalance of conventional military power," Mr. Rumsfeld added.

Mr. Rumsfeld spoke after receiving full honors on the Pentagon grounds on his last day of work there. The ceremonies began with a 19-gun salute before he walked the grounds to inspect the representatives from all the service branches gathered in formation and in full dress.

The ceremony brought to a close the most controversial tenure for a secretary of defense since that of Robert McNamara, whose record tenure in the job was longer than Mr. Rumsfeld's by a mere 10 days. Like Mr. McNamara, Mr. Rumsfeld leaves a war he helped conceive in the hands of others. And like Mr. McNamara, his record is likely to be dissected and debated for years after his resignation.

Mr. Cheney's declaration that "Don Rumsfeld is the finest secretary of defense the nation has ever had," was in keeping with the tone of the event. Mr. Rumsfeld hired Mr. Cheney to work in the Ford administration. Both men served as White House chief of staff, in the House of Representatives and as secretary of defense. (Mr. Rumsfeld has been secretary of defense twice, the first time for President Ford.)

Their shared post-Sept. 11 conviction that the United States must use strength as a deterrent and pre-emptively strike at those who plan to attack the nation has remained unbowed in the face of setbacks in Iraq.

"In this hour of transition every member of our military, and every person at the Pentagon, can be certain that America will stay on the offensive," Mr. Cheney said. "We will stay in the fight until this threat is defeated and our children and grandchildren can live in a safer world."

Mr. Rumsfeld leaves the Pentagon having overseen two wars, an attack on the Pentagon itself and what he called a "transformation" in the use of force. That involved a switch to smaller fighting units that he said would be nimbler and more effective than larger ones favored in the past — an approach that saw early success in Afghanistan but has faced a more severe test in Iraq.

President Bush praised Mr. Rumsfeld. "There has been more profound change at the Department of Defense over the past six years than at any time since the department's creation in the late 1940s. These changes were not easy, but because of Don Rumsfeld's determination and leadership, America has the best equipped, the best trained, and most experienced armed forces in the history of the world."

Mr. Rumsfeld had the last words of the day, using them to warn against backing down in Iraq. "This is a time of great consequence," he said. "It may well be comforting to some to consider graceful exits from the agonies and, indeed, the ugliness of combat. But the enemy thinks differently."

The Failure of Multiculturalism

Canada has long prized itself on being a model of acceptance and welcoming tolerance. One in five of all Canadians is foreign born, and

Toronto, where a recent terrorist plot was hatched, is one of the most cosmopolitan cities in the world. 100,000 newcomers arrive in Toronto every year.

Canadians consider that their model for immigration is more of a quilt rather than a melting pot, meaning that cultural identities are recognized and honored, rather than asking everyone to assimilate. But in any liberal democracy, including the United States, how do we ensure that there is a common framework, a common set of rules that applies to all? Where Liberalism breaks down is that there have to be principles that are not subject to compromise. Maybe multiculturalism is just a nice idea for people who haven't been bombed yet.

Europeans, like Canadians, are now horrified that some of their citizens apparently do not accept the values of a liberal democracy. Britons couldn't believe that young Muslim youths, born and educated in Britain, could possibly play football one day and go off and bomb the London Underground the next.

Muslims are not becoming more secular just because they have adopted the outward trappings of Western society. Being caught between cultures may make the young more religious as a defense mechanism. Home-grown youths in Western countries, susceptible to the seductive beat of the militant, Islamic drum, are finding romance and adventure in the jihadi cause. There is a new generation of alienated, transnational youths, all connected to the Internet, listening to the same music, wearing the same clothes, and, in some cases, being pulled into the same terrorist chat rooms. Muslim youths, who perceive injustices and humiliations in the Muslim world, are won over to extremism, similar to how idealistic youths were recruited into the Communist Party. They want to change the world and they are attracted to the secrecy and the cult-like training camps that terrorists provide.

The whole jihadi culture has become fad-like and cool. To many impressionable youths, Osama bin Laden is the new Che Guevara. It might be laughable if it didn't have such deadly implications.

NATO and the Taliban

The NATO forces battling resurgent Taliban in southern Afghanistan call to mind the Normandy landing. Once again, mostly Canadian, British and American troops are fighting and dying. Most of the rest of Europe is absent from the fight.

NATO Secretary General Jaap de Hoop Scheffer is desperately seeking an additional 2,500 troops to suppress the Taliban. But with a few exceptions, such as the Dutch and Danes, most NATO members prefer the by now traditional division of labor: The Anglo-Saxons do the fighting while the others compete for popularity as armed aid workers.

The 2,900 German troops in Afghanistan are concentrated in the relatively safe north, focusing on reconstruction. France may withdraw its 200 special forces and opposes American plans for NATO to establish stronger links with like-minded countries outside the alliance. Most NATO members, including Italy, France and Spain, have placed absurd restrictions on their troops in Afghanistan. Some can operate only in calm regions; others won't fight in winter. These limits partly reflect the insufficient training and equipment of many European armies. While the U.S. spends about 4% of GDP on defense, the European average is half that.

Whatever the reason, this resistance to committing the troops and funds necessary to defeat the Taliban hardly matches the rhetorical commitment to the cause. The same NATO partners that refuse to provide adequate resources declare that losing Afghanistan is not an option. And right they are. If the Taliban are allowed to re-establish Afghanistan as global jihad's international headquarters, Europe would probably suffer more than the U.S. or Canada. The terrorists are opportunistic killers, attacking where there is the least resistance. Since September 11, they have failed to carry out another attack on U.S. soil. Scores have died in bomb attacks in Europe.

Afghanistan is both a test case for the West's resolve in the fight against Islamic terror and portent for the future of NATO. It is supposedly the "good" war, the multilateral war, the war that even the United Nations approved. If NATO can't muster the forces to defeat the remnants of al-Qaeda's original state sponsor, what is it good for?

U.N. Budget Excesses

Secretary General Ban Ki-moon's proposed "initial" budget for 2008-09 is $4.2 billion, a 15% increase over the Secretariat's current budget. Then include the $4.8 billion for the additions the Secretary General has already identified. But even that is not the final figure. The U.N. budget is released piece by piece; the full budget will end up being in excess of $5.2 billion, a 25% increase over the last two-year budget cycle of 2006-07.

Mr. Ban's proposed increases aren't going for humanitarian assistance in Darfur or development aid to Africa. Roughly 75% is for salaries and other staff costs - in other words, toward boosting the size of the U.N. bureaucracy. Peacekeeping goes on a separate budget, which is anticipated to grow 40%, to $7 billion from $5 billion.

The U.S. is the largest donor to the U.N., paying roughly one-quarter of its budget. With the support of Japan, the second-largest donor, the U.S. is asking that the U.N. set budget priorities Mr. Ban's proposed budget is the largest increase in the history of the U.N. For a body that still hasn't implemented many of the reforms proposed by Paul Volcker's Oil for Food report, this budget should be unacceptable to every major donor.

Liberal Failure

What have the Democrats accomplished since winning Congress?

Their campaign promises are unfulfilled. Democratic leadership is in disarray and Congress's approval rating has fallen to its lowest point in history.

The Democrats have made clear all their talk about fiscal discipline is just talk. They' are proposing to spend $205 billion more than even the President has proposed over the next five years.

If the Democrats roll back the president's 2001 and 2003 tax cuts, every income-tax payer will pay more as all tax rates rise. Families will pay

$500 more per child as they lose the child tax credit. Taxes on small businesses would go up by an average of about $4,000. Retirees will pay higher taxes on investment retirement income. Even worse is the $1 trillion tax increase proposed as tax reform by the Democrats' chief tax writer.

Beholden to MoveOn.org and other left-wing groups, Democratic leaders have ignored the progress made in Iraq by the surge, diminished the efforts of our military, and wasted precious time with failed attempts to force an immediate withdrawal from Iraq. They continue to try to implement this course, which would lead to chaos in the region, the creation of a possible terror state with the third largest oil reserves in the world, and a major propaganda victory for Osama bin Laden as well as for Iran, Hamas and Hezbollah.

After promising on the campaign trail to "support our troops," Democrats tried to cut off funding for our military while our soldiers and Marines are under fire from the enemy. Fortunately 19 Senate Democrats voted against their own leadership's proposal. Democrats also tried to stuff an emergency war-spending bill with billions of dollars of pork for individual members. The party's leaders then stalled an emergency supplemental bill with funding for body armor, bullets and mine-resistant vehicles.

Democrats pledged a "Congress that strongly honors our responsibility to protect our people from terrorism". Instead, they have refused to make permanent reforms of the Foreign Intelligence Surveillance Act that the Director of National Intelligence said were needed to close "critical gaps in our intelligence capability." Their presidential candidates have pledged an end to the Terrorist Surveillance Program.

Senate Democratic leaders, thinking there was an opening for political advantage, slow-walked the confirmation of Judge Michael Mukasey to be the next attorney general. Delaying his confirmation only made it harder to prosecute the war.

Democrats promised "civility and bipartisanship." Instead, they stiff-armed their Republican colleagues, refused to include them in budget negotiations between the two houses, and have launched more than 400 investigations and made more than 675 requests for documents, interviews or testimony. They refused a bipartisan compromise on an expansion of the State Children's Health Insurance Program, instead wasting precious time sending the president a bill they knew he would veto. They did so knowing that they would not be able to override that veto as they calculated that putting the children's health-care program at risk would score political points.

The list of Congress's failures grows each month - no energy bill, no action on health care no action on the mortgage crisis, no immigration reform, no progress on renewing "No Child Left Behind" and inaction on appointment of judges and on reducing trade barriers.

Democrats reflexively look for short-term partisan advantage and attempt to appease the party's most strident Liberals. The Democratic victory in 2006 was narrow. They won the House by 85,961 votes out of over 80 million cast and the Senate by a mere 3,562 out of over 62 million cast. A party that wins control by that narrow margin can quickly see its fortune reversed when it fails to act responsibly, fails to fulfill its promises, and fails to lead.

Vietnam Revisited

Operation Frequent Wind ended on April 30. Marine helicopters evacuated the last U.S. personnel from the embassy in Saigon, hours before communist tanks rolled into the city. Thousands of desperate Vietnamese gathered at the embassy gate and begged to be taken with them. Others committed suicide.

This outcome was the inevitable result of the USA deciding to cut and run. Two of the three presidential candidates are proposing to do just that yet again in Iraq.

The U.S. had won the war in Vietnam on the battlefield, just as the surge has done today in Iraq. Over Easter 1972, South Vietnamese forces, backed by U.S. airpower, crushed the last communist offensive, killing nearly 100,000 North Vietnamese troops.

The North was forced to sign peace accords in Paris recognizing the Republic of South Vietnam. It was a fragile but sustainable peace, with an elected government in Saigon that was growing stronger every month. With 160,000 North Vietnamese soldiers still in South Vietnam, keeping the South free required continuing US help, especially air support and military equipment to discourage the North attacking again. Instead the last 2,500 U.S. support troops went home.

US Liberals had had enough. Much like Iraq today, the vast majority of South Vietnam had been pacified. Its government was taking on difficult but essential political changes, including land reform. The Democratic-controlled Congress, wanted no part of it. They assumed failure in Vietnam would complete their rout of the hated Richard Nixon, who was already out of office thanks to Watergate, and position them for victory in the 1976 presidential election.

The American public had been conditioned by the Liberal media to see Vietnam as a failed policy, and taught that America was in the middle of a civil war which the Vietnamese had to sort out themselves. Once the last American troops left Vietnam, public opinion would never tolerate re-entry into a war widely seen as a blunder and endless quagmire.

In early 1975 the communists launched a massive attack. President Gerald Ford asked for $1 billion in supplemental funds to help the South Vietnamese, and Congress refused. They had already pulled the plug on the U.S.-supported government of Lon Nol in Cambodia. Ford had no choice but to order the evacuation of remaining U.S. personnel.

After nearly two decades of devastating war and 58,000 American combat deaths, the U.S. left Southeast Asia. As the last helicopter lifted off from Saigon, the New York Times published an article with the title, "Indochina without Americans: For Most, a Better Life." They asked, "What future could possibly be more terrible than the reality of a war that had cost so much in lives and treasure?"

The North Vietnamese Communists soon provided the answer. At least 65,000 Vietnamese were murdered – the equivalent in terms of Vietnam's population at the time, of killing three-quarters of a million people in today's U.S. The new communist regime ordered at least a third of South Vietnam's population to pass through its re-education camps, where 250,000 died of disease, starvation and brutal working conditions. The last inmates were not released until 1986.

Cambodia's fate was even worse. At least one and a half million Cambodians were butchered or starved to death in the Khmer Rouge's killing fields and re-education camps, put to death by a fanatical regime that believed anyone who wore eyeglasses must have "bourgeois intellectual tendencies" and must be shot.

The scale of moral collapse and suffering went beyond Indochina. The pullout had a domino effect on U.S. power and prestige. Marxist-Leninist regimes emerged not only in Vietnam, Cambodia, and Laos, but in Ethiopia and Guinea Bissau (1974), Madagascar, Cape Verde, Mozambique, and Angola (1975), Afghanistan (1978), and Grenada and Nicaragua (1979). Soviet troops were welcomed in Fidel Castro's Cuba for the first time since the 1962 missile crisis. Cuban troops traveled freely to Africa to prop up Marxist regimes there.

In 1979 the Ayatollah Khomeini was able to establish his brutal theocratic rule over Iran, confident that America, having learned the lessons of Vietnam, would never intervene.

In Iraq, US Liberals are once again ready to show that the USA is wanting when put to the test.

Great Presidents – Bush and Lincoln

Like all great leaders, President George W. Bush has the courage of his convictions, despite all the naysayers and despite being unpopular as a consequence. Abraham Lincoln was cut from the same cloth.

Five years have passed since the horrific attack on our American homeland, and, still, there is one serious, undeniable fact we have yet to confront: We are, today, not where we wanted to be and nowhere near where we need to be.

In April of 1861, in response to the firing on Fort Sumter, President Lincoln called for 75,000 volunteers to serve for 90 days. Lincoln had greatly underestimated the challenge of preserving the Union. No one imagined that what would become the Civil War would last four years and take the lives of 620,000 Americans.

By the summer of 1862, with thousands of Americans already dead or wounded and the hopes of a quick resolution to the war all but abandoned, three political factions had emerged. There were those who thought the war was too hard and would have accepted defeat by negotiating the end of the United States by allowing the South to secede. Second were those who urged staying the course by muddling through with a cautious military policy and a desire to be "moderate and reasonable" about Southern property rights, including slavery.

We see these first two factions today. The Kerry-Gore-Pelosi- Reid – Clinton - Obama bloc declares the war too hard, the world too dangerous. They try to find some explainable way to avoid reality and promote a policy of weakness and withdrawal abroad.

Most government officials constitute the second wing, which argues the system is doing the best it can and that we have to "stay the course" -- no matter how unproductive. Just consider the following: Osama bin Laden is still at large. Afghanistan is still insecure. Iraq is still violent. North Korea and Iran are still building nuclear weapons and missiles. Terrorist recruiting is still occurring in across the planet.

By late summer, 1862, Lincoln agonizingly concluded that a third faction had the right strategy for victory. This group's strategy demanded reorganizing everything as needed, intensifying the war, and bringing the full might of the industrial North to bear until the war was won.

The first and greatest lesson of the last five years parallels what Lincoln came to understand. The dangers are greater, the enemy is more determined, and victory will be substantially harder than we had expected in the early days after the initial attack. Despite how painful it would prove to be, Lincoln chose the road to victory. President Bush today finds himself in precisely the same dilemma Lincoln faced 144 years ago. With American survival at stake, he also must choose. His strategies are not wrong, but they are failing. And they are failing for three reasons.

(1) They do not define the scale of the emerging World War III, between the West and the forces of militant Islam, and so they do not outline how difficult the challenge is and how big the effort will have to be. (2) They do not define victory in this larger war as our goal, and so the energy,

resources and intensity needed to win cannot be mobilized. (3) They do not establish clear metrics of achievement and then replace leaders, bureaucrats and bureaucracies as needed to achieve those goals.

To be sure, Mr. Bush understands that we cannot ignore our enemies; they are real. He knows that an enemy who believes in religiously sanctioned suicide-bombing is an enemy who, with a nuclear or biological weapon, is a mortal threat to our survival as a free country. The analysis Mr. Bush offers the nation -- before the Joint Session on Sept. 20, 2001, in his 2002 State of the Union, in his 2005 Second Inaugural -- is consistently correct. On each occasion, he outlines the threat, the moral nature of the conflict and the absolute requirement for victory.

Unfortunately, the great bureaucracies Mr. Bush presides over (but does not run) have either not read his speeches or do not believe in his analysis. The result has been a national security performance gap that we must confront if we are to succeed in winning this rising World War III.

We have to be honest about how big this problem is and then design new, bolder and more profound strategies to secure American national security in a very dangerous 21st century. Unless we, like Lincoln, think anew, we cannot set the nation on a course for victory. Here are some initial steps:

First, the president should address a Joint Session of Congress to explain to the country the urgency of the threat of losing millions of people in one or more cities if our enemies find a way to deliver weapons of mass murder to American soil. He should further communicate the scale of the anti-American coalition, the clarity of their desire to destroy America, and the requirement that we defeat them. He should then make clear to the world that a determined American people whose very civilization is at stake will undertake the measures needed to prevail over our enemies. While desiring the widest possible support, we will not compromise our self-defense in order to please our critics.

Then he should announce an aggressively honest review of what has not worked in the first five years of the war. Based upon the findings he should initiate a sweeping transformation of the White House's national security apparatus. The current hopelessly slow and inefficient interagency system should be replaced by a new metrics-based and ruthlessly disciplined integrated system of accountability, with clear timetables and clear responsibilities.

The president should insist upon creating new aggressive entrepreneurial national security systems that replace (rather than reform) the current failing bureaucracies. For example, the Agency for International Development has been a disaster in both Afghanistan and Iraq. The president should issue new regulations where possible and propose new legislation where necessary. The old systems cannot be allowed to continue to fail without consequence. Those within the bureaucracies who cannot follow the president's directives should be compelled to leave.

Following this initiative, the president should propose a dramatic and deep overhaul of homeland security grounded in metrics-based performance to create a system capable of meeting the seriousness of the threat. The leaders of the new national security and homeland security organizations should be asked what they need to win this emerging World War III, and then the budget should be developed. We need a war budget, but we currently have an OMB-driven, pseudo-war budget. The goal of victory, ultimately, will lead to a dramatically larger budget, which will lead to a serious national debate. We can win this argument, but we first have to make it.

Congress should pass an act that recognizes that we are entering World War III and serves notice that the U.S. will use all its resources to defeat our enemies -- not accommodate, understand or negotiate with them, but defeat them.

Because the threat of losing millions of Americans is real, Congress should hold blunt, no-holds-barred oversight hearings on what is and is not working. Laws should be changed to shift from bureaucratic to entrepreneurial implementation throughout the national security and homeland security elements of government.

Beyond our shores, we must commit to defeating the enemies of freedom in Iraq, starting with doubling the size of the Iraqi military and police forces. We should put Iran, Syria and Saudi Arabia on notice that any help going to the enemies of the Iraqi people will be considered hostile acts by the U.S. In southern Lebanon, the U.S. should insist on disarming Hezbollah, emphasizing it as the first direct defeat of Syria and Iran -- thus restoring American prestige in the region while undermining the influence of the Syrian and Iranian dictatorships.

Further, we should make clear our goal of replacing the repressive dictatorships in North Korea, Iran and Syria, whose aim is to do great harm to the American people and our allies. Our first steps should be the kind of sustained aggressive strategy of replacement which Ronald Reagan directed brilliantly in Poland, and ultimately led to the collapse of the Soviet empire.

The result of this effort would be borders that are controlled, ports that are secure and an enemy that understands the cost of going up against the full might of the U.S. No enemy can stand against a determined American people. But first we must commit to victory. These steps are the first on a long and difficult road to victory, but are necessary to win the future.

How War Can Bring Peace

Offensive action abroad has protected the homeland. Our military presence in Afghanistan and our aggressive policies around the globe have seriously disrupted the enemy. Through a mix of military and paramilitary action, pre-emptive strikes, deterrent threats and surveillance we have captured many terrorist leaders, destroyed training camps and structures of communication and control, and uncovered valuable intelligence troves.

Liberals maintain that such offensive action feeds resentment and spawns more terrorism. But if aggression can create resentment, passivity and defensiveness can inspire contempt. Our weak responses to al-Qaeda attacks on the Khobar Towers, the African embassies and the destroyer Cole, and our withdrawal from Somalia, emboldened the enemy and allowed it to organize and train for the 9/11 attacks.

Going forward, we should more vigorously embrace technology as a tool for taking the fight to the Islamic terrorists. The same technological changes that help terrorists plot to deliver weapons of mass destruction, including low-cost information and communication over the Internet, also make it easier for the government to monitor and pre-empt terrorist plots. US Liberals overreact to the new technology, stoking fears of an Orwellian surveillance state. But properly designed programs can produce large gains in security in return for small losses of privacy and liberty. The price is well worth it.

Thank you President Bush

How much international terrorism has been forgotten and how little credit the president has received for keeping Americans safe.

Everyone on 9/12/2001 and thereafter – in New York City and in cities across America – was quite certain that the next terrorist strike was imminent. The stock market collapsed on such fears. We endured interminable delays at airport security checkpoints. Our fears were no longer isolated to skyscrapers – from now, all aspects of daily life would evoke terror. We would come to familiarize ourselves with the color-coded scale of threat conditions issued by the Department of Homeland Security. (Was it safe to go out on orange, or did we have to wait until yellow?)

Each American city adopted its own visions of trauma. There were new categories of vulnerable public spaces. Our worst terrorism nightmares were projected onto local landmarks: Rodeo Drive, the Sears Tower, the French Quarter, River Walk, the Golden Gate Bridge, the Space Needle. Suddenly, living in rural, outlying areas seemed like a sensible lifestyle choice.

We all waited for terrorism's second shoe to drop, and, seven years later … nothing has happened in the USA … yet.

Other cities around the world became targets: Madrid, Glasgow, London and Bali; the entire nation of Denmark; and, of course, Jerusalem and Tel Aviv. Here in America, the focus moved from concerns over counterterrorism measures and the abuse of presidential authority to the war in Iraq, the sub prime mortgage crisis, the failing economy, the public meltdown of Britney Spears, and now, the presidential elections.

All this time Americans have been safe from suicide bombers, biological warfare and collapsing skyscrapers, while the rest of the world has been on red alert. And yet President Bush is regarded as the worst president in American history?

Liberals maintain that our involvement in Iraq, Afghanistan and Israel has rendered America even less safe and that the President has further radicalized our enemies and alienated our nation. They expand this theme by postulating that the animosity for America now, improbably, runs even deeper. The resentments and aspirations which gave rise to 9/11 have grown and so no one should draw comfort in the relative safety of our shores.

Liberals fail to explain how the extraordinary success of al Qaeda on 9/11/2001, has not been repeated in the following seven years.

The only possible explanation is that we have been successful in thwarting and disabling al-Qaeda's operations. The aggressive measures the President took, and the unequivocal message he sent, have worked. As a consequence, Liberals have the luxury and freedom of being able to hate him.

Had there been another terrorist attack or, even worse, a dozen more in cities all over America – a fear that was real on 9/12/2001 – would Liberals have quarreled over legally suspect counterterrorism measures?

Terrorism is now largely off the table in the minds of most Americans. As a consequence, President Bush's greatest achievement has been denied to him by people who ungratefully avail themselves of the protection that his Administration has provided. It will be left to others, in the rear view mirror of history when the USA has experienced what comes after the Bush Administration, to conclude how much we owe to George Walker Bush.

CHAPTER 19
LOOKING FORWARD

Republican Scorecard

Despite Republican control of the White House and of the Senate and House until recently, federal spending increased 45 percent under Republican governance since 2001 and government has become more intrusive in the everyday lives of Americans. We have still not resolved retirement funding or the appropriate size and scope of government. Meanwhile, even the Bush tax cuts have yet to be made permanent.

Republicans need to return to the vision that inspire their voters and gave them a majority — lower taxes, less government, more freedom. Reining in federal spending, reforming a broken tax code, passing realistic immigration reform and creating an ownership society through entitlement reform are ideas that resonate with voters. When conservatives abandon limited government principles, credibility with voters is lost.

The Bush tax cuts will terminate within three years. The $1,000 per child tax credit will drop to $500, marriage-penalty relief goes away, and all income tax rates go up. Republicans have vowed to make the tax cuts permanent. Democrats have pledged to reverse them.

Democrats have no Plan. Whether it was the nuclear freeze, opposition to the liberation of Kuwait, or their cut and run proposals in Iraq, Democrats choose wrongly on foreign policy and defense. The USA needs to win in Iraq and we'll be victorious if we act long-term. Democratic control will lead to retreat. Democrats provide ineffective governance particularly in a time of change, instability and war. They are the party of big government and value power over principle.

Unfortunately too many US voters want to repeat the embarrassment of Vietnam, rather than stay the course in Iraq. Saddam Hussein was guilty of crimes against his own people and guilty of mass murder. It was right that he was deposed and hanged but that means little to US voters. All that they know is that the going is too tough in Iraq and when the going gets tough, US voters want to get out. That mind set opens the door to Liberals.

Behaving like Republicans

Becoming Republicans again will require us to come to grips with what has ailed the GOP party – namely, the triumph of big-government Republicanism. All that compassionate conservatism achieved was to convince the American people to elect the party that was truly skilled at Liberal government: the Democrats.

Compassionate conservatism's starting point had merit. The essential argument that Republicans should orient policy around how our ideas will affect the poor is indisputable. Yet conservatives are conservatives because their policies promote deliverance from poverty rather than dependence on government. Spending increases and entitlement expansion are not the answer. Spending other people's money is not compassionate.

Regaining the Republican brand as the party of fiscal discipline will require them to rejoin the real world of budget choices and priorities, and to leave behind the fantasyland of borrowing without limits. Instead of adopting earmarks, each Republican can adopt examples of government waste, largess and fraud, and restart the permanent campaign against big government.

Republicans can tear up the "emergency spending" credit card and refuse to accept any new spending whatsoever, including for the wars in Iraq and Afghanistan, until Congress does its job of eliminating wasteful spending. The federal budget contains a vast unexplored area of offsets and earmarks.

Congress is a club of dishonest and unprincipled people who ensure their own re-election by bringing home the bacon to their own constituencies. Since almost everyone indulges in this pork barrel spending, the result is fiscal disaster. Most Republicans are little better than Democrats. A few Republicans tried to limit the spending bills for Fiscal Year 2007 presented by a Congress controlled by Democrats, by attempting to strip out all special-interest earmarks. The withdrawal shakes won out as most Members contemplated a year without pork and the prospect of having to find a real job outside Congress (or to enter the lucrative world of being a lobbyist) if the voters were dissatisfied that they did not deliver enough free hand-outs. So the usual mutual back scratching prevailed in their exclusive club where they spend other peoples' money for their own job security.

The 2007 agriculture bill, for example, included a new $4.9 billion emergency handout for farmers, courtesy of North Dakota Democrat Kent Conrad. Millions more were directed to Alaskan salmon research, Montana sheep, New York geese and animal-waste management in Kentucky. The 10 remaining Senate spending bills (and nine in the House) contained some 12,000 earmarks. Liberals like to wrap them all into one giant omnibus bill whose innards no one is able to inspect. Dishonest and unprincipled members of both Houses of Congress, whether they are Republicans or Democrats are then happy; that label applies to almost all of them.

Democrats Then and Now

In 1935, President Franklin D. Roosevelt signed the Social Security Act into law. It released senior citizens from the fear of want. In 1965, President Lyndon B. Johnson signed into law Medicare and Medicaid, the second most significant improvement in health security for older Americans. President Johnson's Great Society program focused on: aid to education, attack on disease, Medicare, urban renewal, beautification, conservation, development of depressed regions, a wide-scale fight against poverty, control and prevention of crime and delinquency, and removal of obstacles to the right to vote. In a more civil and cooperative era, Congress rapidly enacted Johnson's recommendations.

The traditional strength of the Democratic Party, until 1964, was the alliance between the political machines of the big-city ethnics groups and the segregationist South. President Johnson, by ensuring the passage of the civil rights acts, unwittingly sacrificed that alliance for the greater good of the country. The South is now Republican as are successful immigrants and their children like Sam Alito. They have benefited from and support the great opportunities of our society which come from conservative ideology.

The Democratic Party has been hijacked by Liberals such as the Kennedys. As a palliative for their own wealth, obtained by nefarious means, they have sought to attack and discredit conservatives and their ideals and to inflame those who have not achieved the American dream, so that Liberals might bolster their power and influence.

Liberal Democrats have been ineffective and increasingly hostile to Republicans and the US Capitalist system. It is now Republicans who have inherited the true mantle of Roosevelt and Johnson.

As medical research has developed a broad spectrum of lifesaving drugs, Medicare beneficiaries are confronted with drugs that are unaffordable to many. The new Medicare prescription drug program to address this issue was introduced by President Bush.. It marked the most significant change in federal health policy for seniors since 1965. Liberals opposed George Bush and tried to stop this initiative.

Pension reform is desperately needed. Each year the predicament for future generations becomes worse as people live longer. George Bush championed this reform and was rebuffed aggressively by Liberals.

Judge Alito promised to judge using "the rule of law" as his guide and so Liberals attacked him. They want someone who will judge through their prism and will give the social outcomes they desire. Liberals want someone who will champion their causes, such as abortion rights, affirmative action, homosexual rights increased welfare and bigger Government.

The Return of the Liberal Dwarfs

John Edwards, the former Democratic senator from North Carolina and vice presidential nominee, failed in taking his second run at the White House. Edwards made his fortune pocketing a major part of the proceeds as a contingency lawyer arguing for excessive punitive damages in class action suits in civil liability cases.   His platform now is unionization, as a recent article in the Boston Globe propounded -

"Thirty million American workers, 1 out of every 4, make less than $8.70 an hour. These workers, even the ones who work full time year-round, do not earn enough to lift a family of four out of poverty. Whole industries are exporting high-wage jobs to other nations and millions of Americans are struggling at two or three jobs and still finding the middle class out of reach. We have a moral responsibility to help those who are doing everything they can to get by, but are still stuck at jobs with poverty wages.

The hotel industry employs more than 1.3 million people. Hotel chains are finding the money to invest in their image, their grounds, and their rooms, while wages for hotel workers remain far too low. About 90,000 workers in the hotel industry are represented by the union UNITE HERE. We are launching the "Hotel Workers Rising" campaign. Our goal is to build a broad coalition of hotel workers, community activists, religious leaders, political leaders, and people of conscience to encourage the hotel industry to raise wages."

John Edwards has selected an industry which cannot send its jobs overseas to reduce costs as a platform for his activism. Higher wages will increase the already sky high hotel costs in cities like Boston, increasing business travel expenses, which will force ailing businesses to cut costs elsewhere in order to compete globally. The result will be lost jobs in these businesses and more hotel vacancies, which will mean lost jobs in the hotel industry also. For these reasons hotel industry executives of conscience will not raise wages without corresponding productivity gains. Meanwhile if John Edwards wanted to do something useful, he would find ways to get better value out of the huge amounts the USA wastes on its inadequate education so that the working poor could lift themselves economically. He would also want to remove disincentives like welfare dependant and entitlement attitudes which sap workers' desire to improve their lot in life, since there is an inadequate reward for really working smart instead of going through the motions and free loading. As Russians used to say under communism – "You pretend to pay us and we pretend to work."

Unfortunately Senator Barack Obama and Senator Hillary Clinton are Liberal Dwarfs also.

US Foreign Policy

Our focus must be on worldwide capitalism and not democracy. India and China will both overtake the USA in Gross National Product in the next 30 years. We can no longer afford our profligate ways.

44% of Britons work for government or rely on welfare for over half their income. The USA is headed in the same direction.

We have to get our own house in order with our politicians cooperating in international affairs. We need to see the type of relationship that Bush Senior and Clinton developed on Tsunami relief applied to international business. Our efforts to promote democracy are misrepresented and misunderstood, throughout the world. We cannot afford these burdens in an ungrateful world. We should let the United Nations do its job and the United Nations bear the consequences. US aid should all be spent on expansion of US business interests. Microsoft's $2 billion to be spent in India over the next four years is how we can do the most good.

Nations and nationalism will have declining significance. The big multinationals will have greater power and significance than nations as individual countries lose their importance. Individuals must be prepared to travel and live where the action is. This race will be won by the USA. Almost all Private Equity Companies are home grown. What we have to avoid is more disasters like the US car industry.

It is our companies and not our armies that will bring civilization to the world. Only when people have jobs and possessions to acquire and defend will they have a real interest in peace and greater prosperity. They need to soften their passions for Islam, rise above their myopic concepts and learn to engage in global capitalist development.

Radical Islamists harnessed indignation over the Danish Cartoons to further their political goals and their theocratic ends by fomenting hatred for the West and for moderate regimes in the Muslim world. Any voices of moderation in the Muslim world are the ones that are being intimidated and silenced. Those few journalists and leaders who have spoken out against the rioting have been vilified and assailed, and even jailed. 11 journalists in five Islamic countries face prosecution for printing some of the Danish cartoons, even when their purpose was to condemn them. This reaction is that of cowed authorities appeasing Fundamental Islamists. It is time for the USA to let these people sort out their own problems in their own countries.

The USA succeeds because of the power of individual entrepreneurial activity which is only possible in a truly open democracy. Business triumphs over government inadequacies. If we play to our capitalist strengths, we will defeat our own Liberals, save the USA for future generations and do most good in the world.

Sowing Democracy

US Liberals have the mistaken belief that sowing democracy worldwide is the bounden duty of the USA. By agreeing with them, President Bush achieved their support when they elected him to a second term as President. "It is the policy of the United States to seek and support the growth of democratic movements and institutions in every nation and culture, with the ultimate goal of ending tyranny in our world," he said in his second inaugural address.

Democracy is difficult to spread and impossible to impose on people who believe that they can achieve everlasting life in paradise by indiscriminate mass murder. Democracy entails a willingness to share power and give up power.

In the real world there will always be a need for allies who are not democratically elected. The Bush administration has found that Hosni Mubarak in Egypt and Pervez Musharraf in Pakistan are simply too important as allies to denigrate, even though democracy in their countries is not real.

The Bush administration has backed Somalia's warlords in the hopes that they could keep an Islamic government from power.

Democratization is not necessarily the best way to fight Islamic extremism. Most states that attempt to transition from autocracy to democracy get stuck in a kind of in-between state. Electoral democracy does not necessarily imply true democracy, especially in the Islamic world.

President Bush has stressed that democracy must come to undemocratic countries wrapped in, and shaped by, the culture and mores of that particular society. In this regard, he understands what Liberals do not want to understand which is that other peoples should not be remade in their image.

For democracy to succeed in Iraq in the foreseeable future, it will require partition into three sovereign states – the same solution as Yugoslavia. Unfortunately that is not what a democratically elected Congress in the USA wants to see happen and President Bush has no alternative but to go along with them if he wants adequate funding to keep our troops in Iraq.

Be Patient and Stay the Course.

Good, real change has to evolve. Forces trying to prevent meaningful change in the body politic are always formidable and revolution brings its own set of problems, which are often worse than what came before. In this regard see romanticized accounts of history as just that. A good example is the American Revolution as taught in the USA. Much of it is romanticized claptrap. The birth of America as a free nation came about because of excessive taxation of the few wealthy British colonials and enough support in the motherland to let the USA go the way its leaders wanted for their own self interest. It was an unpopular civil war for Britain when it had its hands full in what was to become the final defeat of France after centuries of fighting. Wars, civil war in particular, seem to be an inevitable pre-cursor to the birth of democratic nations. The Middle East and Africa have been and will continue to be no different. Interference from US Liberal and European do-gooders makes the situation worse.

Learn Well

US Politics is all about domestic power. The world in dispute is not understood or of genuine importance. US Politicians are obsessed with promoting the concept of democracy. It is of paramount importance in US foreign policy even if the recipients of US interference cannot handle democracy.

The historical low rating of Congress is well deserved. The USA should do better than the self-serving, self-aggrandizing, pork barrel junkies that are attracted to Washington. Of concern also is that our Presidential system only attracts a weak field of candidates. The next President is decided by how well money talks and on media manipulation.

If you want information go the Internet. The last reliable newspaper is the Wall Street Journal and we should fear for that now that Murdoch has his hands on it. In particular do not believe what you read in the New York Times or see on CBS, NBC, ABC, BBC or CNN.

Senator McCain as the Republican Nominee for President

Senator McCain voted against President Bush's tax cuts and a constitutional amendment banning same-sex marriage, He fought for looser immigration rules. He privately criticized Supreme Court nominee Justice Samuel A. Alito Jr. because "he wore his conservatism on his sleeve" and only reluctantly reached out to free market conservatives. Senator McCain is weak in his knowledge of business economics and does not understand that it is the Capitalist engine which drives everything.

Black Racism

Black Racism in the USA is a major problem. White racism is not. The beginning of the end of white racism occurred around 1960, as TV images gave instant publicity throughout the USA. Most whites were disgusted. Martin Luther King climbed on the band wagon. He did not initiate it. The same was the case in Rhodesia and South Africa. White Rhodesians and South Africans brought an end to apartheid even though they knew that they would be the losers. Why? It was because racism was repugnant to most whites in these countries.

Black racism could be the deciding factor in the next Presidential election, which is alarming. If Barack Obama is elected, it is because he is the choice of more than 92% of blacks, many of whom support him because he is not white. That is black racism.

Income disparity between whites and blacks has increased since the civil rights movement and affirmative action. More free handouts lead to dependency and more free handouts. Many blacks gravitate to the worst stereotypes and adopt the hip hop lifestyle of their lowest common denominator, instead of reaching for success.

The Upbringing of Barack Obama

All that the media reports is a glossed-over fairy tale about Barack Obama's upbringing. Obama's father had children by four women and abandoned each of them in succession. Time Magazine reported that Obama's mother Sam Ann Soetoro decided not to follow Obama's father back to Kenya, neatly overlooking the fact that he was returning to Kenya (and his Kenyan wife and children) with an American wife whom he had married in Massachusetts after he left Sam Ann and Barack in Hawaii to take advantage of a free education at Harvard University.

Obama's mother was named Sam because her father, an itinerant furniture salesman was disappointed that she was not a boy. Sam also had an itinerant lifestyle and became Soetoro when she married an Indonesian student at Hawaii University and went with him to live in Indonesia. That is where Obama spent most of his early formative years trying to grapple with an alien culture where he was viewed as an American negro oddity and was so called even though he was half white and his black father only ever surfaced very briefly once more in Barack's life. His mother often made unfortunate choices and impetuous decisions, living often on welfare. She spent most of her life in Indonesia even though she divorced her Indonesian husband after she gave birth to an Asian biracial half sister for Obama.

The saving of Obama was when he was given a financial scholarship to an elite prep school in Hawaii and thereafter lived with his white grandparents who raised him with his mother largely absent. She chose instead to be a perpetual student eventually receiving a doctorate degree when she was 49.

Life with a Flower Child White Mother

On Feb. 2, 1961, several months after they met, Obama's parents got married with no friends or relations in attendance in Maui, even though his black father was already married to a woman back in Kenya. At that point, Sam Ann was 18 and three months pregnant with Barack Obama II. She dropped out of the University of Hawaii after one semester. Within a year, his father left for Harvard to get a PhD in economics to round out his free US education before returning to Kenya. He only ever surfaced once more for a few days in Obama's life, much later. Except for having half his genes from a black man, Barack is anything but black. Sam Ann collected food stamps and relied on her parents to take care of young Barack. She became sexually intimate with another foreign student, Lolo Soetoro, at the University of Hawaii and eventually married him in 1967 and took Obama to live with him in Indonesia.

Lolo's house, on the outskirts of Jakarta, was much different from the high-rises of Honolulu. There was no electricity, and the streets were not paved. Inflation was running at more than 600%, and everything was scarce. White Sam Ann and her son, considered by the locals to be a large American Negro were the first foreigners to live in the neighborhood, populated with much human misery - children without limbs, men with leprosy.

In 1971, when Obama was 10, he went back to Hawaii to live with her parents and attend Punahou, an élite prep school where he had been accepted on a financial scholarship obtained by his grandparents. A year later, Sam Ann also went back to Hawaii, taking her daughter but leaving her husband behind. Ann's husband visited Hawaii frequently, but they never lived together again. Ann filed for divorce in 1980.

After three years of living with her children in a small apartment in Honolulu, subsisting on student grants, Ann went back to Indonesia leaving Obama behind in Hawaii to be raised by his grandparents. Every so often, Ann would leave Indonesia to live in Hawaii, New

York and Pakistan. She and her daughter sometimes lived in garage apartments and spare rooms of friends.

Obama's Grandmother

Madelyn Dunham is now 85 and lives on her own in an apartment in Waikiki. Soetoro-Ng, Obama's half-sister, who is a teacher, visits her grandmother daily.

Madelyn Payne was born and raised in Kansas. She married Stanley Dunham in 1940. She was an aircraft inspector for Boeing during World War II. After the war, she attended UC-Berkeley but did not graduate. She joined the Bank of Hawaii in 1960 when she came to the Islands with her husband. She started in the bank's escrow department, became its manager in 1962 and eventually was named the bank's first woman vice president in 1970, along with another person. She retired in 1986. Stanley Dunham died in 1992 at the age of 73.

Obama's Inexperience

Obama does not connect with blue-collar white Democrats.

An even bigger problem is his ill-informed replies on critical foreign policy questions, which he then adjusts when his naivety is exposed. His ability to shift his ground quickly is reminiscent of Bill Clinton. When will the real Obama stand up? Indeed is there a real Obama? He is a white man with 50% black genes, who chose to marry a black woman and passes himself off as black. He chose as his spiritual leader a charismatic black preacher who spews out anti-white anti-government rhetoric. That served him well with the black community to jump start and sustain his political career but he will now distance himself from these positions with the presidency almost within his grasp.

It is on foreign policy that his innate intelligence is not enough to save him from showing that he is totally ill-equipped to be commander-in-chief. He has been dismissive of the threats posed by Iran, North Korea, Venezuela, Cuba and Syria. That's the same Iran arming and training insurgents and illegal militias in Iraq to kill American soldiers; that is supporting Hezbollah and Hamas in violent attacks on Lebanon and

Israel; and that is racing to develop a nuclear weapon while threatening the annihilation of Israel.

Is North Korea, the world's worst nuclear proliferator an insignificant threat? Is Venezuela simply reactionary rather than an adversary willing to destabilize the hemisphere? Will he ignore the Castros' willingness to aid revolutionary movements? Does he not understand Syria's meddling in Lebanon and support for terrorism by Hamas and Hezbollah?

Obama has proclaimed his willingness to meet without precondition with the leaders of Iran, Syria, North Korea, Venezuela and Cuba. He insists that he would only be doing what Richard Nixon did by going to China. Obama seemingly does not know that there were 134 private meetings between U.S. and Chinese diplomats and 18 months of behind-the-scenes discussions before Kissinger secretly visited Beijing. Seven more months of hard work followed before Nixon went to China.

The Chinese didn't change because of a presidential visit. China was induced to want to join the community of nations less by the prospect of dialogue with the United States than by fear of being attacked by its ostensible ally, the Soviet Union.

The same is true with other successful negotiations. President Ronald Reagan prepared the ground for his meetings with a series of Soviet leaders by rebuilding the U.S. military, restoring confidence in American intentions, and pressuring the Soviets by raising the specter of a missile defense shield. He effectively bankrupted the Communist regime by exposing their inability to keep up with US capitalist economic superiority.

Reagan knew that rogue states only change when they see there are real consequences of their actions, and when it is in their interest to change. This change requires patience, vision, hard work and the use of all the tools, talents and relationships available to the USA. A recent example was when Libya, fearful of American resolve after 9/11, gave up its chemical, biological and nuclear weapons programs, all more advanced than Western intelligence thought.

Reagan knew that he must not squander the prestige of the American presidency and the authority of the United States by meaningless meetings that serve only as propaganda victories for our adversaries. Obama seems to believe charisma and smooth talk can fundamentally alter the behavior of Iran, Syria, North Korea, Venezuela and Cuba.

One of Iran's top foreign policy goals is a precipitous U.S. withdrawal from Iraq. That is Obama's top foreign policy goal, too. Iran and other rogue states will not alter their behavior if Obama gives them what they want, without preconditions.

Obama is hopelessly out of his depth on national security as his lack of understanding of foreign policy shows.

Obama's Media Army

The media is not allowed to ask questions Barack Obama does not want to address, without the Liberal media rushing to his defense by demonizing the questioners. After a debate moderated by ABC, who are unabashedly Liberal, their even more Liberal colleagues in the media were outraged. Next day, they let their feelings be known.

- "Akin to a federal crime . . . new benchmarks of degradation," The New Yorker's Hendrik Hertzberg declared, of the debate.

- "Despicable. . . . slanted against Obama," Washington Post critic Tom Shales charged.

- A "disgusting spectacle," the New York Times's David Carr opined.

- The questions had "disgraced democracy itself," according to columnist Will Bunch of the Philadelphia Daily News.

Part of the debate went as follows –

From the Democratic debate on ABC (April 2008) :

CHARLES GIBSON: You have however said you would favor an increase in the capital gains tax. As a matter of fact, you said on CNBC, and I quote, "I certainly would not go above what existed under Bill Clinton, which was 28%." It's now 15%. That's almost a doubling if you went to 28%. But actually Bill Clinton in 1997 signed legislation that dropped the capital gains tax to 20%.

BARACK OBAMA: Right.

GIBSON: And George Bush has taken it down to 15%.

OBAMA: Right.

GIBSON: And in each instance, when the rate dropped, revenues from the tax increased. The government took in more money. And in the 1980s, when the tax was increased to 28%, the revenues went down. So why raise it at all, especially given the fact that 100 million people in this country own stock and would be affected?

OBAMA: Well, Charlie, what I've said is that I would look at raising the capital gains tax for purposes of fairness. We saw an article today which showed that the top 50 hedge fund managers made $29 billion last year – $29 billion for 50 individuals. And part of what has happened is that those who are able to work the stock market and amass huge fortunes on capital gains are paying a lower tax rate than their secretaries. That's not fair.

And what I want is not oppressive taxation. I want businesses to thrive and I want people to be rewarded for their success. But what I also want to make sure is that our tax system is fair and that we are able to finance health care for Americans who currently don't have it and that we're able to invest in our infrastructure and invest in our schools. . . .

GIBSON: But history shows that when you drop the capital gains tax, the revenues go up.

OBAMA: Well, that might happen or it might not. It depends on what's happening on Wall Street and how business is going. I think the biggest problem that we've got on Wall Street right now is the fact that we've got a housing crisis that this president has not been attentive to and that it took John McCain three tries before he got it right. And if we can stabilize that market and we can get credit flowing again, then I think we'll see stocks do well, and once again I think we can generate the revenue that we need to run this government and hopefully to pay down some of this debt.

Obama holds a special place in the hearts of a good part of the media, a status ensured by their shared political sympathies and his star power. That status has in turn given rise to a tendency to provide generous explanations, and put the best possible gloss on missteps and utterances seriously embarrassing to Obama.

Offered a chance to explain the meaning of his remarks about the reasons people living in small towns cling to guns and religion, he goes on to repeat them all over again in different words. That is what he thinks and no amount of Liberal spin will change what he thinks and who he is, until Obama confronts himself. We can only hope that learning experience does not occur while he is in the White House.

David Gergen, senior CNN commentator, weighed in just after the first explosion of reports on Obama's long time pastor, spiritual advisor and friend, Jeremiah Wright, in an attempt at exculpation for Obama. About this spiritual leader – whose sermons declared the September 11 attacks to be America's just deserts, who instructed his flock that the United States had set forth on a genocidal program to kill black Americans with the AIDS virus, who held forth as gospel every paranoid fantasy espoused by the lunatic fringe about America's crimes – Gergen said, "Actually, Rev. Wright may love this country more than many of us . . . but we've fallen short."

Obama is unable to confront, forthrightly, the pastor's poisonous pronouncements and his own relationship with him. He has the same problem in confronting his relationship with middle aged former terrorist bombers, still proud of what they did to an extent that they feel to this day that they did not do enough.

Liberals celebrated Obama's speech on race where he attempted to point the finger in the opposite direction saying that Wright was no worse as a racist than his white, loving grandmother, who did more than anyone to give Obama the opportunity to be where he is to-day. How cowardly and despicable is that?

Obama, the Media's Choice

Senator Obama is often an indifferent speaker without a teleprompter. He has large gaps in his knowledge base, and is just as likely to dig in and embrace a policy misstatement as abandon it.

Obama erroneously claimed that his uncle helped liberate the Auschwitz concentration camp. His revised claim was that his great uncle helped liberate Buchenwald. Previously in 2002, Obama claimed his grandfather knew U.S. troops who had liberated Auschwitz and Treblinka – even though only Russian troops entered those concentration camps. The media let it all pass.

For such lies, Hillary Clinton would have been given a much rougher ride by the media and John McCain would have been flagellated. That is because gaffes are often blown up or downplayed based on whether or not they further a story line the media has attached to a politician.

When John McCain claimed that Sunni (as opposed to Shiite) militants in Iraq are being supported by Iran, coverage of the alleged blunder tracked back to his age and stamina. (In fact, Iran may well be supplying both Sunni and Shiite militants.) Dan Quayle, tagged with a reputation as a dumb blond male, never lived down his misspelling of "potatoe."

Barack Obama, has largely been given a pass, even when he suggested that America has 57 states, and his arrogant claim in a Memorial Day speech that America's "fallen heroes" were present and listening to him in the audience.

Last year he said that his birth was inspired by events there which took place four years after he was born out of wedlock when his mother was infatuated with a Kenyan, already married who quickly moved on to other conquests.

He denied last April that it was his handwriting on a questionnaire in which, as a state senate candidate, he favored a ban on handguns. His campaign now contends that, even if it was his handwriting, this doesn't prove he read the full questionnaire.

Obama has contended that Iran doesn't "pose a serious threat to us," saying that "tiny countries" with small defense budgets aren't much to worry about. He presumably does not know that Iran has a quarter of the population of the USA, is well on its way to developing nuclear weapons and has leaders who hate Israel to the extent of wanting to wipe them from the face of the earth. Obama is managed by people who quickly correct him. Next day, Obama declared that he had "made it clear for years that the threat from Iran is grave." He has said he would meet with Venezuelan dictator Hugo Chávez to discuss, among other issues, Chávez's support of the Marxist FARC guerrillas in Colombia.

The next day, he insisted any country supporting the FARC should suffer "regional isolation."

Obama pledged to meet, without precondition, the leaders of Iran, North Korea, Syria and Cuba. He called President Bush's refusal to meet with them "ridiculous" and a "disgrace."

Heavily criticized, Mr. Obama dug in rather than backtrack. He's claimed, in defense of his position, that John F. Kennedy's 1961 summit with Soviet leader Nikita Khrushchev in Vienna was a crucial meeting that led to the end of the Cold War.

Kennedy himself admitted he was unprepared for Khrushchev's bullying. "He beat the hell out of me," Kennedy confided to advisers. The Soviet leader reported to his Politburo that the American president was weak. Two months later, the Berlin Wall was erected and stood for 28 years. Does Obama not know what happened between 1961 and 1989

Over the years, reporters have tagged a long list of conservative public figures, from Barry Goldwater to Ronald Reagan to George W. Bush, as dim and uninformed.

No leading Liberal figure has developed a similar media reputation, even though the likes of Al Gore, John Kerry, Harry Reid and Nancy Pelosi have given good reason to question what they have between their ears. To this list we can now add Barack Obama.

The Clinton Phenomenon

The core Democratic Party never did like Bill Clinton's New Democrat ways, but after Walter Mondale and Michael Dukakis they needed his epic political gifts to win back the White House.

The price was that they had to put their ethics in a blind Clinton trust. Whitewater and the missing billing records, Webb Hubbell, cattle futures and "Red" Bone, the Lincoln Bedroom, Johnny Chung and the overseas fund-raising scandals, Paula Jones and lying under oath, Monica and the parsing of words, using power for sexual gratification while not having sex, just being with a dependant person who had sex with Bill that was not reciprocated by him. Bill Clinton left office after

2000 amid the tawdry pardons. George W. Bush's main campaign theme in 2000 was restoring "dignity" and "honor" to the Oval Office, and Al Gore lost despite two-thirds of voters saying the U.S. was moving in the right direction. William Safire, declared that "everybody in politics lies," but the Clintons "do it with such ease, it's troubling."

Hillary Clinton had also won a Senate seat that year, and she had presidential ambitions of her own. As the Bush years rolled on and John Kerry lost, they watched Hillary build her machine and plot a Clinton restoration. They watched, too, as the New York Senator did her own triangulating on Iraq, first voting for it, actively supporting it before turning against it as the election neared. Party regulars fell in line behind her, and her nomination was thought to be inevitable.

Then a new star emerged in Barack Obama, a man who had Bill Clinton's political talent and Hillary's liberal dogma. He had charisma, a flair for raising money, and he held out the chance of a 2008 Democratic landslide and perhaps the revival of a Liberal majority, circa 1965. He became the new darling of the Liberal media. Liberals were 'shocked' to see the Clintons play the race card in South Carolina. (Blacks do it constantly and biracial people, like Obama spin themselves as black, but woe betides any mention of race by a white person). The media played up their secrecy over tax records and Clinton Foundation donors, while columnists were appalled to hear her assail Brack Obama for his associations with radical bomber William Ayers. By the time Hillary Clinton made her claim about dodging Bosnian sniper fire, Democrats and their media friends no longer called it a mere gaffe. This time the remark was said to be emblematic of her entire political career. The Democratic establishment who had believed her about Whitewater and the rest now claimed she never tells the truth about anything.

As the scales suddenly fell from Liberal eyes, the most striking statistic was the one in exit polls. Asked if they considered Mrs. Clinton "honest and trustworthy," no fewer than 50% of Democratic primary voters in North Carolina said she was not. In Indiana, the figure was 45%.

Hillary Clinton finally conceded. By staying in the race and reminding us who Obama really is to the extent that anyone knows, she is helping her candidacy for 2012, which is very Clintonian behavior.

The USA and France

In Europe, the French view tends to be most at odds with the aberrant folk who elected George W. Bush.

In recent decades, good Americans have included John F. Kennedy and his wife Jackie (whose supposed elegance betrayed a European sensibility), Woody Allen (of European urbanity and wit), Michael Moore (of European vehemence on the Iraq war) and Al Gore (of European environmentalism).

Now, in French eyes, there is a new good American, namely Barack Obama. His book, "The Audacity of Hope," is a best seller. His face is everywhere, sometimes in socialist realist images evoking Che Guevara.

Out in the troubled suburbs, with their large African and Arab populations and broad mistrust of a political system that has produced one black parliamentarian among the 555 representing mainland France, Obama is an urban legend. In France at least, he has high-low appeal.

France is not alone in its Obama fever — German infatuation is scarcely less intense and across Europe, Obama is strongly favored to cut the USA down to size.

The French delight in Obama's talk of dialogue, even with Iran. They think, wrongly as it happens, that Obama is just like them, but until the media creation is overtaken by reality, the euphoria will continue.

The USA as the Enemy

The perception of the United States has improved in most countries over the past year, driven largely by the fact that George Bush will soon be leaving office and he is likely to be replaced by a person who portrays himself as more black than white, even though that person is an unknown quantity outside of media creativity.

Many across the globe blame the United States for slumping economies and global warming. Europeans are still much more negative than they were at the beginning of the decade, and highly negative views prevail in the Muslim world. But the world sees the possibility of change to their advantage with the prospect of a new president who they perceive to be more like them.

They have greater confidence in Senator Barack Obama, the presumptive Democratic nominee, than in his Republican rival, Senator John McCain, "to do the right thing regarding world affairs." This feeling is strongest in Europe, Australia, Japan and Tanzania, which borders Kenya, the homeland of Obama's father, who abandoned him in infancy.

China is now considered by the masses to be ascendant in world affairs. Many people - including 3 out of 10 Americans - think that China will eventually replace the United States as the world's leading superpower. China though is seen as even worse than the USA in ignoring the interests of other countries and is faulted on matters related to the environment and human rights.

China feels good about itself. 86 percent are satisfied and the number is rising. In the United States, where 70 percent are dissatisfied with the way things are going, pessimism extends beyond the economy to the country's chief foreign policy challenge: only a minority of Americans (40 percent) now think efforts to establish a democratic government in Iraq will succeed. In 2006, a majority (54 percent) still believed that success was likely.

When asked which country is hurting the environment, most people around the world cite the United States with people also increasingly pointing fingers at China. In turn, the United States and China are among the 10 countries where majorities do not define global warming as a very serious problem.

The survey of 24,717 people is the seventh major study conducted by the Pew Global Attitudes. In only eight countries surveyed by Pew do majorities have a favorable view of the United States: Britain, India, Lebanon, Nigeria, Poland, South Africa, South Korea and Tanzania. In one-third of the survey countries, more respondents see the United States more as an enemy than as a partner. This view is especially strong in Turkey, a NATO ally, and in Pakistan, a partner in Washington's efforts to fight terrorism.

EPILOGUE

War on Terrorism

A total withdrawal from Iraq would play into the hands of the jihadist terrorists. As Osama bin Laden's deputy, Ayman al-Zawahri, made clear shortly after 9/11 in his book "Knights Under the Prophet's Banner," Al Qaeda's most important short-term strategic goal is to seize control of a state, or part of a state, somewhere in the Muslim world. "Confronting the enemies of Islam and launching jihad against them require a Muslim authority, established on a Muslim land," he wrote. "Without achieving this goal our actions will mean nothing." Such a jihadist state would be the ideal launching pad for future attacks on the West.

US Liberal pussyfooting fits all too neatly into Osama bin Laden's master narrative about American foreign policy. His theme is that America is a paper tiger that cannot tolerate body bags coming home; to back it up, he cites Vietnam and, more recently, President Clinton's decision in the early 1990s to pull troops from Somalia. A unilateral pullout from Iraq would only confirm this analysis of American weakness among his jihadist allies.

Islam is being used to persecute people who have other religious beliefs, not only in Muslim countries but also in the West. We need a different response to their behavior. Diplomacy is not the way and we cannot negotiate with terrorists. We are also running out of time as the war on terror is increasingly unacceptable to Liberals in Europe. Military body bags are now as ill received in Europe as they are in the USA and relatively low civilian casualties are treated as catastrophic. We hand terrorists a victory every time there is any publicity as everything is now played out in the full glare of the Liberal media. In increasingly antiwar America, similar dynamics are at work.

How much international terrorism has been forgotten and how little credit the president has received for keeping Americans safe. Liberals fail to explain how the extraordinary success of Al Qaeda on 9/11/2001, has not been repeated in the following seven years.

The explanation is that we have been successful in thwarting and disabling al Qaeda's operations. The aggressive measures the President took, and the unequivocal message he sent, have worked. As a consequence, Liberals have the luxury and freedom of being able to hate him as other cities around the world became targets: Madrid, Glasgow, London and Bali; the entire nation of Denmark; and, of course, Jerusalem and Tel Aviv.

Iraq

Iraq's active WMD program had been destroyed, mostly by U.N. weapons inspectors, sometime in the 1990s, but Saddam Hussein maintained a pretense of having those weapons mainly to keep Iran at bay and maintain his standing in the world.. Saddam's admission that an Iraqi WMD program remained a threat so long as Saddam remained in power could not be ignored. Sanctions were increasingly ineffective as many countries challenged them with dozens of unauthorized flights into Iraq.

Bowing to this reality, the Bush Administration came to office promising to ease the sanctions regime, even as it spent billions patrolling the so-called "No-Fly Zones." And as we learned after the invasion, Saddam was well on his way to breaking free of the sanctions by bribing everyone from a British member of parliament to a former French cabinet minister, all through a U.N. convenience known as Oil for Food.

Saddam acknowledged that he gave the order to use chemical weapons against Kurdish civilians, the dictator acknowledged that he had given the orders personally and explained himself in a word: "Necessary."

It was necessary to depose Saddam Hussein. It would have been morally reprehensible not to have done so. Justice was served when he was tried in an Iraqi Court and hanged.

President Bush on Iraq

If we pull our military out, we will be handing Iraq over to our worst enemies - Saddam's former henchmen, armed groups with ties to Iran, and al-Qaeda terrorists from all over the world who would suddenly have a base of operations far more valuable than Afghanistan under the Taliban.

"The war we fight today is more than a military conflict. It is the decisive ideological struggle of the 21st century. The violence in the Middle East and the recently thwarted attack to blow up planes over the Atlantic Ocean are part of the same movement that resulted in the Sept. 11 attacks.

Despite their differences, these groups form the outline of a single movement, a worldwide network of radicals that use terror to kill those who stand in the way of their totalitarian ideology. And the unifying feature of this movement, the link that spans sectarian divisions and local grievances, is the rigid conviction that free societies are a threat to their twisted view of Islam.

They are successors to fascists, to Nazis, to communists and other totalitarians of the 20th century. And history shows what the outcome will be. This war will be difficult. This war will be long. And this war will end in the defeat of the terrorists.

The Resolve to Win

We have the capability to win in the Middle East. The only question is whether we have the resolve.

President Lincoln faced the same dilemma as George Bush, as will the next President. George W Bush had the same qualities as Abraham Lincoln.

Just as then, we have to choose between resolve and retreat, with no guarantees about how it will end. All we can be sure of is that the stakes once again are liberty and decency versus tyranny and terror. We are fighting an enemy that feeds on weakness and expects us to lose heart. The world for generations to come will remember if we flinch.

Will he next President be equal to the challenge?

Hate in Politics

Major damage occurs when hate is directed against our President. The Liberals' hatred is so strong that they are seemingly indifferent to the consequences of portraying our elected Leader as a half wit. They are telling the world that we were all stupid in electing him and that he should be treated with contempt. Their hatred is based on lies about George Bush's IQ, integrity, character, oratory and beliefs. They insult not only George Bush, but more importantly the USA, since we chose him through our democratic processes. By so doing, they threaten the security and well being of all of us. The world community feels that they can treat us with contempt.

Hollywood has taken to glorifying suicide bombing and terrorism under the guise of seeking understanding. They depict suicide bombers not as evil, but likeable humans. In their casting, the bomber characters are heroes deserving of our sympathy. Hollywood explains that they are seeking to portray the underlying human personality. What they are doing is depicting Western norms of personality. They have no way of looking into or understanding the depraved, tortured and twisted minds of Islamic suicide bombers and how they are being duped and brainwashed by fanatics such as al-Qaeda and Hamas. Hollywood has become another propaganda vehicle, just like the Liberal media for our enemies to use.

CNN's former news executive, Jordan Eason, acknowledged after the fall of Saddam Hussein that his network had long sanitized its news from Iraq, since reporting the unvarnished truth "would have jeopardized the lives of our Baghdad staff." The Islam fascists are emboldened by appeasement and submissiveness. The BBC, CNN, New York Times, Boston Globe and all their fellow travelers betray ideals that generations of Americans and Britons have died to defend.

What we need is not appeasement and apologies and a dread of giving offense by our Liberal media. We must not be intimidated by bullies and must face down fanatics. In the global struggle against Islamist extremism, we need a media voice of courage that leads the way. Our

Achilles heel is the broad distribution worldwide of the Liberal Media with no other channels for us to get out the truth.

The Liberal Media justifies the actions of our enemies, by casting them as victims and by labeling the Bush Administration as villains, lunatics, liars, power hungry war mongers and delusional incompetents. US Liberals empower our enemies and endanger the USA.

By undermining US foreign policy, US Liberals have removed any options that we have for preventing Iran from developing a nuclear weapons capability. All of our efforts should now be directed at assessing when they will have this capability and what dominoes will fall as a result. For starters both Saudi Arabia and Turkey will also develop a nuclear bomb. The United Nations will continue to tie US hands through meaningless resolutions that no one will enforce. Iran knows that we are powerless. We should stop appearing to be naïve by pretending that we have the resolve to thwart them. The unintended consequence of the ongoing conflict in Iraq is that Liberals now have control in the USA. For their part, the Iranians will press on. Iran is a broken society over which the mullahs rule. The danger posed by Iran has not been exaggerated.

There is a yearning for Democratic and Republican lawmakers to reduce their extreme partisanship, look for common ground instead of attacking one another, and start working together to solve some of the problems that affect us all. Years of slash-and-burn politics for selfish or ideological reasons have exhausted the patience of the nation and driven down its faith in government to get things done for the public good.

Do not hold your breath as this rapprochement will not happen any time soon. Indeed US Liberals do not have the stomach for world leadership and its inevitable difficulties. Liberals cannot tolerate uncertainty or a competitive environment and are ready to circle the wagons and live in isolation.

Anti-Bush pathology runs so deep among many Liberals that they really do think they are grappling with a potential fascist situation in our own Administration. Liberals overblown concerns about civil rights, profiling and privacy and their road blocks to real security screening still leaves us vulnerable to be blown out of the skies.

World View

One-third of countries see the United States more as an enemy than as a partner. This view is especially strong in Turkey, a NATO ally, and in Pakistan, a partner in Washington's efforts to fight terrorism.

The USA has repeatedly saved Europe from itself. The USA was a critical factor in ending World War 1 and the key factor in winning World War 2. The USA then defeated communism.

The USA pushed the UK into Europe. That was the end of the special relationship. To-day the UK is stuck somewhere between The European Union and an independent Island entity of decreasing importance saddled with its own declining recognition of the greatest Empire ever. At its height, Great Britain ruled a quarter of the world and the sun never set on the British Empire. To-day the British Empire is an embarrassing memory for UK Liberals to explain away.

Sixty-five percent of Britons consider Americans vulgar; 72% think American society is unequal; 52% take a negative view of American culture; and 58% believe the U.S. is an essentially imperial power, one that wants to dominate the world by one means or another.

Our focus must be on pursuing worldwide capitalism. India and China will both overtake the USA in Gross National Product in the next 30 years. We can no longer afford our profligate ways. 44% of Britons work for government or rely on welfare for over half their income. The USA is headed in the same direction.

China feels good about itself. 86 percent are satisfied and the number is rising. In the United States, 70 percent are dissatisfied; pessimism extends beyond the economy to the country's chief foreign policy challenges: only a minority of Americans (40 percent) now think efforts to establish a democratic government in Iraq will succeed.

Whenever the leader of another country is visiting the White House, his treatment by the US Liberal Media is always the same. He stands there ignored while the President is asked questions that are intended to embarrass him and have nothing to do with our visitor.

The same happens when an American political leader is abroad – but in reverse. Condoleezza Rice is embarrassed by the US Liberal Media in every European country she visits, with her counterpart from that country standing silently by her side.

US Liberals think that we are so much more important than any other country that they do not even need to show any interest in that country.

USA in Trouble

The Fiscal mess in the USA is a major reason for President Bush's unpopularity but its causes are principally outside his control. Nevertheless the USA and many Americans are not doing well and the President is blamed.

We have lost our moral compass and are in free fall. We are obsessed with all sorts of unhealthy desires and vices which we are unwilling to deny or even curb. Our institutions such as marriage between one man and one woman for life, have largely collapsed. We have an intractable lawless black underclass which has opted out of our established society, at least 12 million illegal aliens, huge debts and a profligate life style, which cannot be maintained for the majority, as living standards rise in the rest of the world. We are increasingly a free hand out society with the few supporting the many.

Our tax system has now become an inefficient tool to attempt to redistribute wealth with the most wealthy able to find loopholes and the burden falling on those who are upwardly mobile, reducing their motivation to stay in the earned income pool in the USA, as they see their hard work disproportionately benefiting those who contribute nothing but problems to our society. In 2005, the richest 1% paid about 39% of all income taxes. The richest 5% paid 60%, and the richest 10% paid 70%. These tax shares are all up substantially since 1990, and even somewhat since 2000. Meanwhile, Americans with an income below the median - half of all households - paid only 3% of all income taxes in 2005.

The United States spends a great deal of money on education but has still lost its standing as the country with the highest college graduation rate in the world. (South Korea has passed us and Japan, Britain and Canada are close behind.) Many blacks in particular drop out of High School and an extraordinary number graduate to prison at huge cost to the rest of us. Many black girls in particular become single parent low income or non-earners costing tax payers dearly.

Black racism is a major problem in the USA. Almost all will vote for Obama since he has positioned himself as their candidate; in fact he is biracial, abandoned by his black father, a not uncommon occurrence, largely brought up by his white grandparents in relative opulence in a prestigious private school in Hawaii after his 'flower child' white mother also had a brief marriage to an Indonesian and lived in a relatively poor Muslim environment in Indonesia, where Obama experienced intolerance towards what they considered to be an American black child. To-day, Obama educated in the Ivy League is 'whiter' than almost all people in the USA.

Spending on physical infrastructure is at a 20-year high as a share of gross domestic product, but too much of the money is spent on the inefficient pork barrel programs championed by individual members of Congress to ensure their re-election. Congress is populated with second raters and their hangers-on, who are hopelessly corrupt.

Health care is considered to be an entitlement particularly by those who are less wealthy. Treatment options and associated costs are ever expanding but the only people who have the wherewithal to pay for everyone, are the wealthy, through increased taxation. The USA has by far the most expensive health care in the world with Corporations and the minority of higher earning tax payers being expected to foot the entire bill.

Prolonged dollar weakness has created a multitude of problems. Companies have to devote an increasing portion of their time and energy to currencies rather than their operating business. Foreigners, not always friends, are gaining wealth relative to Americans. Rather than making the U.S. more competitive, the dollar's weakness makes it harder to justify investments in the U.S., where growth is slowing and interest rates are higher than in Europe or Japan to compensate for the weakening dollar. The investment killer is that assets in the U.S. keep losing value in foreign-currency terms, so U.S. opportunities have to be significantly better to entice investment in the face of a weakening dollar.

The Importance of Family Values

When I visited the Library of George Bush Senior, what struck me most forcibly was what a thoroughly decent person he is and how the Bush family back to his grandparents and Barbara's grandparents are all highly principled people with exemplary family values. As the Senior George Bush described his own father - he gave us love and discipline in equal amounts and a great deal of both.

The Kennedy family, in contrast to the Bush family, is and always has been most dysfunctional. Bill Clinton, John Kerry and Barack Obama all came from a dysfunctional background in their early years. While that should not disqualify these individuals, the potential psychological damage from their childhood years should not be ignored either. Otherwise we find out while they are in the White House. Personality and character are largely formed in the first seven years of life.

It is no accident that two Bushes have been President and there could yet be a third from the same generation as George W.

Presidential Election

What is needed is an election which is race and gender free. Barack Obama and Hillary Clinton have run on both. The black vote beat out the women's vote.

Should we not elect candidates who do not need to play the race and gender cards as otherwise we continue to polarize our society. People like Margaret Thatcher and Condoleezza Rice (if she would run) come to mind. Their qualities and abilities make their race and gender a non-issue.

Obama has no experience to fit him to be President but that is of no concern to woolly minded Liberals, of which there are an extraordinary number. Many educated white Liberals vote for Obama out of a misplaced sense of guilt because they feel that blacks have been victimized on an ongoing basis. It is a do-gooders way of trying to correct their perception of injustice through yet another form of affirmative action. Not only will they elect an unsuitable and unqualified candidate, but Obama is not what he has portrayed in any case. He is essentially a white man in a half black skin who plays on the political advantage of positioning himself as black. That level of dishonesty is of concern in a country where black racism is a major problem. We can now expect him to shift to his white side with the black vote in his pocket, so that he can garner the white working class vote. He will start to involve a relationship with his white grandmother (new found and carefully choreographed to appear otherwise) who raised him and whom he accused of racism when he wanted to deflect his own racism as expounded inconveniently by his spiritual friend and advisor (the so called Reverend Wright).

There are powerful white forces driving the Obama train, carefully staying behind the scenes, for their own political ends. The Liberal Media is solidly behind Obama and they are driving support for him worldwide such is their reach and influence, driven by a world wide desire to cut the USA down to size.

Against this back drop of Liberals trying to feather their own nests, is the disquieting news that nuclear weapons technology of a size small enough to be suitable for terrorists has been extensively sold by a Pakistani expert to undesirable elements worldwide. Will Obama and his Liberal handlers be up to the challenge? Or will we once again let our guard down as we did with Jimmy Carter and again with Bill Clinton, if Barack Obama is elected President and we have Liberal control of Congress?